The Invisible Tapestry:
Culture in American Colleges and Universities

by George D. Kuh and Elizabeth J. Whitt

ASHE-ERIC Higher Education Report No. 1, 1988

Prepared by

Clearinghouse on Higher Education
The George Washington University

Published by

Association for the Study of
Higher Education

Jonathan D. Fife,
Series Editor

Cite as
Kuh, George D., and Elizabeth J. Whitt. *The Invisible Tapestry: Culture in American Colleges and Universities*. ASHE-ERIC Higher Education Report No. 1. Washington, D.C.: Association for the Study of Higher Education, 1988.

Library of Congress Catalog Card Number 88-83281
ISSN 0884-0040
ISBN 0-913317-45–4

Managing Editor: Christopher Rigaux
Manuscript Editor: Barbara Fishel/Editech

The ERIC Clearinghouse on Higher Education invites individuals to submit proposals for writing monographs for the Higher Education Report series. Proposals must include:
1. A detailed manuscript proposal of not more than five pages.
2. A chapter-by-chapter outline.
3. A 75-word summary to be used by several review committees for the initial screening and rating of each proposal.
4. A vita.
5. A writing sample.

Cover design by Michael David Brown, Rockville, Maryland

[ERIC] **Clearinghouse on Higher Education**
School of Education and Human Development
The George Washington University
One Dupont Circle, Suite 630
Washington, D.C. 20036-1183

ASHE **Association for the Study of Higher Education**
Texas A&M University
Department of Educational Administration
Harrington Education Center
College Station, Texas 77843

This publication was prepared partially with funding from the Office of Educational Research and Improvement, U.S. Department of Education, under contract no. ED RI-88-062014. The opinions expressed in this report do not necessarily reflect the positions or policies of OERI or the Department.

EXECUTIVE SUMMARY

The competitive advantage of Japanese business and industry in the 1970s prompted organizational theorists and managers in the United States to examine culture-laden management principles. Predictably, the idea of "culture" management began to appear in the higher education literature. The purpose of this report is to identify and discuss the properties of institutional culture and examine how cultural perspectives have been used to describe life in colleges and universities.

What Are Cultural Perspectives?

A focus on culture implies an attempt to identify beliefs, guiding premises and assumptions, norms, rituals, and customs and practices that influence the actions of individuals and groups and the meanings that people give to events in a particular setting (Geertz 1973). Cultural perspectives encourage coherent interpretations of what seem, in isolation, to be atomistic events. Decision making, planning, resource allocation, personnel evaluation, and institutional renewal strategies, when considered one at a time, sometimes seem trivial or void of meaning. Yet individual acts and events, when thought of as nested patterns of cultural behavior, have a pervasive, far-reaching influence on institutional life. For example, to the casual observer, annual events like the freshman induction convocation and the commencement weekend simply mark beginnings and endings. Such ceremonies, however, also can be viewed as important, unifying rituals through which successive generations of students are socialized and bonded.

Institutional culture presents interesting challenges to scholars and administrators. The term "culture" has been used in a cavalier fashion to address almost any behavior, activity, or process in an institution of higher education. Labeling everything "culture" compromises the level of precision typically expected of social science research. Much of the business literature suggests that "culture" can be intentionally manipulated by crafty administrators, while others assume culture is so deeply embedded in the psyche of a group of people that it cannot be systematically altered.

How Is Culture Defined?

Almost as many definitions of culture exist as scholars studying the phenomenon. In some definitions, shared values and beliefs are emphasized; in others, the role of culture in regulating behavior through accepted rules, norms, and practices is underscored. Because scholars from various disciplines have studied culture, it is not surprising that numerous definitions of culture have been proposed. This report defines culture as *persistent patterns of norms, values, practices, beliefs, and assumptions that shape the behavior of individuals and groups in a college or university and provide a frame of reference within which to interpret the meaning of events and actions on and off the campus.*

What Are the Intellectual Foundations of Culture?
Anthropology and sociology, and allied disciplines like social psychology and communications, all contribute to an understanding of institutional culture. Anthropology, particularly the ideational tradition, emphasizes nonrational aspects of life and the creation and transmission of culture through symbols and mental imagery. Sociology and the sociocultural tradition in anthropology address the rational aspects of a college or university and underscore the importance of formal organizational structures and subcultures in transmitting values and beliefs and influencing the behavior of faculty and students.

**What Are Properties of Culture Found in
Colleges and Universities?**
Institutional culture is both a process and a product. As a process, culture shapes, and is shaped by, the ongoing interactions of people on and off campus. As a product, culture reflects interactions among history, traditions, organizational structures, and the behavior of current students, faculty, and staff. Artifacts are observable manifestations of culture, such as the institutional mission statement, architecture, academic program, language, myths, stories, symbols, rites and rituals, and ceremonials. Culture is also revealed through an examination of espoused and enacted values and the core beliefs and assumptions shared by institutional leaders, faculty, students, and other constituents, such as alumni and parents.

Cultural properties overlap. For example, four discrete but interdependent cultures are said to influence a faculty member's behavior: the culture of the discipline, the culture of the academic profession, the culture of the institution, and the culture of the national system of higher education. In many institutions, particularly large public universities, one or more dominant faculty and student subcultures can be found. The possibility that these four cultures simultaneously interact with subcultures as well as forces from the external environment illustrates the complexity with which researchers and administrators must contend when using cultural perspectives.

How Does an Institutional Culture Form?
An institution's culture reflects to some degree the values and accepted practices of the host society. Culture develops from an interplay between the external environment and salient institutional features, such as an institution's historical roots, including religious convictions of founders (if applicable) and external influences, particularly the support of constituents (alumni, philanthropic sponsors); the academic program; a core faculty group, including senior faculty and administrators; the social environment as determined by dominant student subcultures; cultural artifacts, such as architecture, customs, stories, language, and so on; distinctive themes that reflect core values and beliefs and make up the institution's ethos; and the contributions of individual actors, such as a charismatic president or innovative academic dean.

What Role Do Subcultures Play in the Life of a College?
The meaning constructed from events and actions is influenced by many factors, including one's role (student, faculty member), disciplinary perspective, and interests (teaching, research, service). The influence of a subculture on the behavior of its members is mediated by the institutional context, including size, complexity, and mission, as well as the backgrounds and experiences of individual members.

Two perspectives on faculty culture predominate: (1) academics make up one homogenous profession and share values of academic freedom, individual autonomy, collegial governance, and truth seeking; and (2) academics make up a complex of subprofessions characterized by fragmentation and specialization. The culture of the discipline is the primary source of faculty identity and expertise. Elements of disciplinary culture include assumptions about what is worth knowing and how knowledge is created, about the tasks to be performed and standards for effective performance, and about patterns of professional interaction and publication patterns.

Like faculty subcultures, student subcultures are created through interactions with peers, mediated to a certain extent by institutional structures and processes. Preferred approaches to negotiating persistent problems faced by the group are passed to succeeding generations of students, thereby creating and maintaining a set of beliefs, attitudes, and values shared by many students in a particular institution—one or more dominant student cultures. Dominant student cultures may or may not reflect the values and ideals of the institution as a whole, but they nevertheless exert a significant influence on an institution's culture (Clark 1970).

What Are the Implications of the Cultural Perspective?
Culture is holistic and context bound; thus, the meaning of events and behavior cannot be fully appreciated apart from the institution in which they occur. What appear to be similar events means different things in different contexts. As a consequence, behavior that seems reasonable in one setting may or may not be judged appropriate in another. The following implications for administrators and scholars can be adapted to reflect more accurately the cultural features of a particular college or university:

- To understand and appreciate the distinctive aspects of a college or university, examine its culture.
- The assumptions and beliefs held by individuals and groups in a college or university may be different; thus, interpretations of events and actions and the meanings constructed of them will differ.
- Managing meaning is an important responsibility of leaders.
- A core group of institutional leaders (e.g., senior faculty) provides continuity, which is integral to maintaining a cohesive institutional culture.
- Institutional policies and practices are culture driven and culture bound.
- Culture-driven policies and practices may denigrate the integrity and worth of certain groups.
- Institutional culture is difficult to modify in intentional ways.
- Organizational size and complexity work against distinctive patterns of values and assumptions.

What Methods Are Appropriate for Examining Institutional Culture?
Institutional culture is so complex that even members of a particular institution have difficulty comprehending its nuances. To

describe an institution's cultural properties, methods of inquiry are required that can discover core assumptions and beliefs held by faculty, students, and others and the meanings various groups give to artifacts. Techniques of inquiry appropriate for studying culture include observing participants, interviewing key informants, conducting autobiographical interviews, and analyzing documents.

As higher education scholars and administrators learn more about cultural perspectives, informative studies of institutional culture and the role of subcultures in student learning and development can be expected. Cultural perspectives would be especially useful in studying the experiences of minority faculty and students in predominantly white institutions, processes of faculty governance, student and faculty groups as subcultures, and exemplary colleges. By viewing higher education institutions as cultural enterprises, we may learn how the college experience contributes to divisions of class, race, gender, and age within the institution as well as throughout society, how a college or university relates to its prospective, current, and former students, and how to deal more effectively with conflicts between competing interest groups.

ADVISORY BOARD

CONSULTING EDITORS

Charles Adams
Director, The Inquiry Program
Center for the Study of Adult and Higher Education
University of Massachusetts

Ann E. Austin
Research Assistant Professor
Vanderbilt University

Trudy W. Banta
Research Professor
University of Tennessee

Harriet W. Cabell
Associate Dean for Adult Education
Director, External Degree Program
University of Alabama

L. Leon Campbell
Provost and Vice President for Academic Affairs
University of Delaware

Ellen Earle Chaffee
Associate Commissioner for Academic Affairs
North Dakota State Board of Higher Education

Peter T. Ewell
Senior Associate
National Center for Higher Education Management Systems

Reynolds Ferrante
Professor of Higher Education
George Washington University

J. Wade Gilley
Senior Vice President
George Mason University

Judy Diane Grace
Director of Research
Council for Advancement and Support of Education

Madeleine F. Green
Director, Center for Leadership Development
American Council on Education

Milton Greenberg
Provost
American University

Judith Dozier Hackman
Associate Dean
Yale University

Paul W. Hartman
Vice Chancellor for University Relations and Development
Texas Christian University

James C. Hearn
Associate Professor
University of Minnesota

Evelyn Hively
Vice President for Academic Programs
American Association of State Colleges and Universities

Frederic Jacobs
Dean of the Faculties
American University

Paul Jedamus
Professor
University of Colorado

Joseph Katz
Director, New Jersey Master Faculty Program
Woodrow Wilson National Fellowship Foundation

George Keller
Senior Vice President
The Barton-Gillet Company

L. Lee Knefelkamp
Dean, School of Education
American University

David A. Kolb
Professor and Chairman
Department of Organizational Behavior
The Weatherhead School of Management
Case Western Reserve University

Oscar T. Lenning
Vice President for Academic Affairs
Robert Wesleyan College

Charles J. McClain
President
Northeast Missouri State University

Judith B. McLaughlin
Research Associate on Education and Sociology
Harvard University

James L. Morrison
Professor
University of North Carolina

Sheila A. Murdick
Director, National Program on Noncollegiate-Sponsored
 Instruction
New York State Board of Regents

Elizabeth M. Nuss
Executive Director
National Association of Student Personnel Administrators

Robert L. Payton
Director, Center on Philanthropy
Indiana University

Donald M. Sacken
Associate Professor
University of Arizona

Robert A. Scott
President
Ramapo College of New Jersey

Henry A. Spille
Director, Office on Educational Credits and Credentials
American Council on Education

CONTENTS

FOREWORD

The culture of American colleges and universities may be invisible but it is not unobserved. In the 1960s, insightful examinations of the dynamics of higher education such as Becker's *Boys in White* (1961), Feldman and Newcomb's *The Impact of College on Students* (1969), and Hefferlin's *Dynamics of Academic Reform* (1969) all allude to the importance that the organization's culture plays to the functioning of the institution.

Several definitions of culture are offered in this report that help to give meaning to this elusive concept. Essentially, culture is the summation or end-product of all the social and personal values and the consequences of those values that operate within the institution. For example, in a recent report by John Creswell on *Faculty Research Performance* (Report 4, 1985), he points out that young faculty coming from highly productive institutions will soon assimilate the same productivity norms of the institution they join. In other word, if the culture of the institution supports a lesser standard of productivity, it will soon co-opt the previous standard of productivity held by the faculty.

The importance of culture for students is easily seen in the literature that reviews the socialization process in professional schools and the general impact of college on students at the undergraduate level. This literature consistently points out that it is the affective development of a student that has long-term measurable change. This literature also consistently identifies certain institutions as having greater measurable impact on their students than other institutions. Clearly, the distinctive culture of these highly-potent institutions plays a major part in achieving their uniqueness.

Culture also plays a major role in the administration of an institution. Major reversal of a cultural direction may cause institutional disharmony, for example in an institution that has a long history of collegial governance with low individual accountability and maximum autonomy, the faculty may resist any attempts to develop a centralized form of institutional management. For the same reasons, an institution that has a primary value on teaching will initially react negatively to the implementation of a reward system that is based on research productivity.

In this monograph, George Kuh, of Indiana University, and Elizabeth Whitt, of Oklahoma State University, carefully examine the concept of culture. Both administrators and faculty alike can develop policies and procedures that are far more likely to have their desired effects by incorporating the concept of culture. In acknowledging the existing culture and subcultures on a campus and taking them into account when important changes must occur, the leaders of an institution can better ensure successful adoption of their plans and greater acceptance of whatever steps must be taken.

Jonathan D. Fife
Professor and Director
ERIC Clearinghouse on Higher Education
School of Education and Human Development
The George Washington University

ACKNOWLEDGMENTS

We are indebted to many people who were very helpful during the preparation of this report. Participants in the 1987 summer seminar on organizational culture at Indiana University helped us think through many of the complex issues related to cultural perspectives and the place of culture in institutions of higher education. Pat Love assisted in the development of the outline for the manuscript and some of the material in the third section. He also discovered some fugitive literature addressing various aspects of culture that was most useful. For his contributions and gentle criticisms throughout the project, and for his friendship, we are grateful. In addition to her other responsibilities, Connie Riggins produced several drafts of most chapters. Without her good work, we would still be in the rough draft stage. Four anonymous reviewers read the manuscript *very* carefully and made many excellent suggestions. As usual, Jonathan Fife and Christopher Rigaux at the ERIC Clearinghouse on Higher Education were patient and supportive.

Without the material written by hundreds of scholars interested in cultural phenomena, we could not have produced this report. Most of these scholars are included in the list of references. Those most knowledgeable about culture in higher education, however, the premier shapers of culture at colleges and universities all over the country—presidents, academic deans, faculty leaders, student life administrators, and others—are not identified. They know that the examples in the following sections only begin to approximate the deep, pervasive influence of institutional culture on the lives of students and faculty. We salute all those who are actively engaged in maintaining and enriching the culture of their college or university and hope that this report reflects favorably on what they are trying to do.

It would be rash to assume that American colleges have in fact been established for men [and women] for whom the promotion of higher learning was the only or even the main purpose (Bay 1962, p. 983).

Colleges and universities are social communities as well as educational institutions (Hochbaum 1968; Jacob 1957; Sanford 1962b). A stroll across a college campus suggests that faculty and students have a form of life all their own, a culture if you will. The architecture at MIT is obviously different from that at, say, Stanford University. But other institutional features— such as curriculum, academic ceremonies, extracurricular events, and a distinctive language—also distinguish MIT and Stanford from the 3,000 other colleges and universities in the United States. To understand why faculty and students think and behave the ways they do, we must first describe and appreciate their culture (Van Maanen 1979).

Higher education scholars have occasionally used cultural perspectives to learn more about students and faculty in studies ranging from how medical students collaborated to make sense of the faculty's expectations and succeed in medical school (Becker et al. 1961) to an examination of the primary role orientations toward college of different groups of students (Clark and Trow 1966) to a description of ritualistic behavior in one particular student subculture—a social fraternity (Leemon 1972)—to a categorization of faculty according to the degree to which they identified with the cultures of their institution and/ or their discipline (Clark 1963).

This report examines how cultural perspectives can be used to describe, understand, and appreciate college and university life. The plural form of "perspective" suggests that the concept of culture has many different connotations, a point reiterated throughout. This section introduces the concept of culture and explains why a review of the literature on culture in higher education is warranted at this time. It then summarizes conventional and nonorthodox views of institutions of higher education to illustrate the compatibility of cultural perspectives with nonrational views of organizations and concludes with an overview of the remaining sections.

Culture is viewed as an interpretive framework for understanding and appreciating events and actions in colleges and universities rather than as a mechanism to influence or control behavior.

The Warrant for the Report

A rapidly changing external environment (Education Commission 1980; Kerr 1964) poses a threat to the one outcome all colleges have in common—survival (Riesman and Jencks 1962). Economic cycles, state and federal agencies, corporate sponsors, accreditation organizations, and other groups have the potential to significantly influence institutional policy. When times are uncertain, routine organizational responses to systemic changes in the external environment may not be adequate (Cameron 1984; Cameron and Whetten 1983). Under conditions of uncertainty and ambiguity, people usually become more cautious in interpreting the meaning and consequences of their actions (Tierney 1988; Vaill 1984). Cultural perspectives have been proposed as lenses through which the consequences of institutional responses to turbulent, uncertain conditions can be anticipated, understood, even managed (e.g., Dill 1982; Masland 1985; Tierney 1988).

The current interest in using cultural perspectives to understand colleges and universities as organizations was fueled by the success of Japanese manufacturing firms in the 1970s. Many U.S. management consultants enthusiastically embraced the ideas behind Japanese management principles, as described by Ouchi's Theory Z (1981). By the early 1980s, "corporate culture" became *au courant* among organizational development specialists (Salmans 1983). Elements of Japanese management were subsequently introduced into the higher education literature (e.g., Deegan, Steele, and Thelin 1985; Redinbaugh and Redinbaugh 1983).

Not everyone believed Japanese management principles would significantly affect administrative practice in colleges and universities. Wyer (1982) compared Ouchi's ideas with Millett's description (1962) of the collegial model and challenged the notion that Theory Z was an innovative approach to college and university management, pointing out that Theory Z and the classic "collegial" governance model were similar in many respects (e.g., both emphasize participatory management and collaborative decision making). Another researcher argued that culture, an organizational construct, was also broader, deeper, and more complex than the ideas represented in Theory Z (Dill 1982).

Others have attempted to clarify the conceptual confusion between culture and organizational climate and to define culture as an organizational construct for use in theory and practice in higher education (Peterson et al. 1986). No comprehensive work is available that examines how culture has been and can be used to understand college and university life, however.

This report extends the analysis of Peterson et al. by probing more deeply into the properties of culture (e.g., language, rituals, stories, beliefs) and how institutional culture has been portrayed in the higher education literature. Some abuses and potential uses of cultural properties are described, for example, whether institutional culture can be manipulated or controlled, as some have suggested (e.g., Deal and Kennedy 1982; Kilmann et al. 1985).

Culture is viewed as an interpretive framework for understanding and appreciating events and actions in colleges and universities rather than as a mechanism to influence or control behavior. As an interpretive framework, cultural perspectives are "like a rainbow—a 'code of many colors' that tolerates alternative assumptions" (Jelinek, Smircich, and Hirsch 1983, p. 331). In this sense, cultural perspectives acknowledge and legitimate nonrational aspects of college and university life and are incompatible with the myth of organizational rationality.

Organizational Rationality
The study of organizations is rooted in a strong desire for order and orderliness.

Very early in human experience, order seems to have been a kind of inescapable and irretrievable empirical fact. The sun rises and sets; people are born and they die; the seasons come and go; and there is the procession of the stars. The spatial patterning and temporality of man's experience established an imagery of order, forming a backdrop to the drama of cosmos arising out of chaos. In the slow, incremental achievement of a substantial scientific stance with respect to the universe, there had been built into man's semiotic of experience and into his traditional pieties the unquestionable assumption that this is an orderly universe (Meadows 1967, p. 78).

Organizational theory developed to explain how that orderly universe asserted itself in the behavioral settings in which people live, work, and are educated. Organizational models are based on paradigms, on systems of epistemological and ontological assumptions.

[A paradigm] includes a conceptual framework that differentiates the central from other phenomena and delineates the

major components or divisions with the phenomena of inter-est.... [But] the paradigm is more than a conceptual and reasoning structure. It is a form of life, a discourse embed-ded in a social situation, a set of practices.... The paradigm may be seen as a set of rules [that] guides and is sustained by the practices of the community (Benson 1983, p. 36).

Paradigms are useful because they organize thinking in com-plex and ambiguous situations. What appears to be an advan-tage may be a limitation, however, because "the very reason for action is hidden in the unquestioned assumptions of the par-adigm" (Patton 1980, p. 9).

Conventional perspectives on organizing
Views of organizations based on the conventional paradigm have in common assumptions that reflect desire for order and simplicity and promote organizations as rational and efficient (Allison 1971; Chaffee 1983; March and Simon 1958). The characteristics of Weber's ideal bureaucracy (1968)—coordina-tion and control, specialization, and rules for operations and communication—typify the rationality sought and perpetuated by conventional organizational perspectives (Baldridge et al. 1977; Blau 1973). The conventional paradigm continues to dominate thinking about colleges and universities; management by objectives, goal-based planning, organizational charts, com-munication channels, and hierarchical structures demonstrate the sustained belief in organizational rationality.

Organizational rationality is a myth, however (Morgan 1986; see also Meyer 1984). Like primitive myths:

> *[organizational rationality] helps us to see certain patterns of action as legitimate, credible, and normal, and hence to avoid the wrangling and debate that would arise if we were to recognize the basic uncertainty and ambiguity underlying many of our values and actions* (Morgan 1986, p. 135).

Nonorthodox perspectives on organizing
In virtually every discipline (e.g., history, law, economics, psychology, physics), a shift to different ways of apprehending experience is under way (Capra 1983; Ferguson 1980; Gleick 1987; Howard 1985; Kuhn 1970; Lincoln 1985; Schwartz and Ogilvy 1979).

However reluctantly, even the most traditional social think-
ers are now recognizing the distinctiveness of the postindus-
trial world for what truly is an unfolding drama of human
interaction whose potential seems limited or enhanced pri-
marily by our symbolic capacities for constructing meaning-
ful agreements that allow for the committed enactment of
collective life (Cooperrider and Srivastva 1987, p. 133).

The term "demythologizers" describes scholars who use
phenomenology and semiotics as alternative points of view
from which to interpret and explain behavior in the organizational context (Benson 1983). Demythologizers (Burrell and
Morgan 1979; Greenfield 1984; Meyer 1984; and Weick 1979,
for example) have underscored the discrepancy between what
should be and what often *is* in organizations, and they have
fueled the debate between advocates of organizational rationality and those who consider organizations to be nonrational. Demythologizers assert that ambiguity and uncertainty are inherent
in organizational life and that differences between what
"should be" and what is are not evidence of problems that
must be fixed.

To embrace cultural perspectives, one has to suspend belief
in organizational rationality. Thus, those in search of elements
of culture in a college or university must be open to the possibility that such institutions may be nonrational, phenomenological enterprises and must be willing to set aside—or at least
question—conventional assumptions of order and control as
well as the paradigm or world view on which these assumptions are based.

The core of the problem [that people have with the cultural
perspective] may be that Western philosophies and beliefs
are pictures in men's minds as to the nature of what is....
Pictures and explanations are real in one sense because they
are constructions of the human mind and they tell us a lot
about how that mind works as a product of a given culture.
But they are not the mind and they are not the real world
either. They are... "conventions"....If one treats them as
reality, they are impossible to transcend or even to examine
except in their own terms.... Ultimately, what makes sense
(or not) is irrevocably culturally determined and depends
heavily on the context in which the evaluation is made (Hall
1976, p. 188).

For more than 50 years, a conventional paradigm has dominated thinking about and managing institutions of higher education (Clark 1985; Keller 1986; Lincoln 1986)—understandable
because conventional organizational models, when used in con-
cert, account for many important aspects of college and university life. And conventional models are compatible with assumptions that determine the "scientific" study of behavior sup-
ported by the logical positivist inquiry paradigm (Lincoln and
Guba 1985). Although many faculty and more than a few administrators have not studied formal theories of organizational
behavior, they have been influenced by logical positivism and
often interpret actions and events in colleges and universities in
a manner consistent with conventional beliefs and assumptions
(e.g., linear causality). When people do not behave as they are
"supposed to," however, or events come to pass in a way different from that predicted, conventional expectations turn out
not to be very helpful and at times counterproductive.

Perhaps prescriptive ways of thinking about colleges and universities should be set aside in favor of approaches to understanding that "free our minds to see what is there, not what we
think ought to be there, and [that] allow us to derive, or
ground, new theory" (Lincoln 1986, p. 139). Cultural perspectives represent one such approach.

The Remaining Sections
This report examines properties of institutional culture and describes cultural perspectives as lenses for interpreting events
and actions in colleges and universities. In the process, it may
stretch expectations for rationality a bit. Like many aspects of
life, tolerance for ambiguity and curiosity about anomalies are
needed to appreciate cultural aspects of colleges and universities (Cohen and March 1974; Kuh, Whitt, and Shedd 1987;
Lincoln 1985).

The next section, "Culture Defined and Described," discusses the variety of ways culture has been defined and the
complex, multiple properties of culture. In the third section,
"Intellectual Foundations of Culture," the major traditions
within anthropology and sociology focused on the study of culture are summarized to provide a foundation for the following
section, a description of the framework developed for reviewing the higher education literature.

The next section, "Threads of Institutional Culture," offers
illustrations of institutional culture, considering the influence of

structural elements of colleges and universities, such as size and the institution's history, when mapping institutional culture. It also identifies external influences and describes the nature of their effects on culture. The sixth section examines the characteristics of subgroups within faculty, student, and administrative subcultures and considers the interaction among subcultures and their collective influence on the institution's culture. The final section discusses implications of cultural perspectives for faculty and administrators and offers some suggestions for how cultural perspectives can further illuminate college and university life.

CULTURE DEFINED AND DESCRIBED

If there were any word to serve the purpose as well, I would unhesitatingly use it in preference to one that seems at times downright slippery and at other times impossibly vague and all-embracing. But although "culture" has uncomfortably many denotations, it is the only term that seems satisfactorily to combine the notions...of a shared way of thinking and a collective way of behaving (Becher 1984, p. 166).

Certain ideas burst upon the intellectual landscape with such a force that they seem to have the potential to resolve all fundamental problems and clarify all obscure issues facing a field (Langer, cited in Geertz 1973). Cultural perspectives have been widely used in a general, all-encompassing manner to subsume almost every concept, event, or activity that might occur in an organized setting (Deal and Kennedy 1982; Schwartz and Davis 1981). Some (see, for example, Morgan 1986) have suggested that culture is a metaphor for organizations. Because culture lacks conceptual clarity, however, its utility as a metaphor for colleges and universities seems limited, perhaps even confusing. Indeed, unless more precision is achieved, cultural perspectives may obscure more than they reveal. That is, if cultural elements are not more clearly explicated, the insights into college and university life promised by cultural views will be blurred, thus reducing their power and utility (Trice and Beyer 1984).

Risks are inherent, however, in attempting to flesh out or specify the elements of culture. For example, thinking about cultural properties as distinct institutional attributes (e.g., beliefs, stories, norms, and so on) that can be separated and independently analyzed is compatible with conventional assumptions undergirding organizational rationality. The perception that culture can be intentionally controlled does violence to some important properties of culture, such as its complex, holistic character (Geertz 1973), an entity greater than the sum of its parts (Morgan 1986). Nevertheless, when talking about and studying culture, we do separate properties, such as language, from rituals, stories, belief systems, and values. In doing so, however, we must acknowledge the contradiction inherent between analysis and holistic perception and the distortion that results whenever a single element is isolated in the complex web of history, traditions, and patterns of behaviors that have developed in a college or university (Taylor 1984).

The culture of a college or university defines, identifies, and legitimates authority in educational settings.

Toward a Definition of Culture

> *[We] have been entrusted with the difficult task of speaking about culture. But there is nothing in the world more elusive. One cannot analyze it, for its components are infinite. One cannot describe it, for it is Protean in shape. An attempt to encompass its meaning in words is like trying to seize the air in the hand when one finds that it is everywhere except within one's grasp* (Lowell, cited in Kroeber and Kluckhohn 1952, p. 7).

Asked to define the institution's culture, an MIT student, "without batting an eye,...responded by saying: 'It's everything we aren't tested on in the classroom' " (Van Maanen 1987, p. 5). Although most social scientists would not be satisfied with this level of precision, her response is consistent with the myriad meanings and connotations of culture reported in the literature. Indeed, culture cannot be succinctly defined because it is an inferential concept (Cusick 1987), "something that is perceived, something felt" (Handy 1976, p. 185).

Culture is described as a social or normative glue (Smircich 1983)—based on shared values and beliefs (see Pascale and Athos 1981)—that holds organizations together and serves four general purposes: (1) it conveys a sense of identity; (2) it facilitates commitment to an entity, such as the college or peer group, other than self; (3) it enhances the stability of a group's social system; and (4) it is a sense-making device that guides and shapes behavior. In addition, the culture of a college or university defines, identifies, and legitimates authority in educational settings (Gage 1978; Goodlad 1984). Therefore, studies of institutional culture have implications for policy and strategies for institutional change (Elmore 1987).

Most definitions of culture convey one or more of the following properties (Schein 1985): (1) observed behavioral regularities (Goffman 1959, 1961; Van Maanen 1979), such as the hours faculty spend in the office; (2) norms (Homans 1950) or specific guides to conduct, some of which (e.g., mores) are more salient than others (Broom and Selznick 1973); (3) dominant values espoused by the organization (Deal and Kennedy 1982), such as the importance of inquiry in research universities and the commitment to undergraduate teaching in liberal arts colleges; (4) the philosophy that guides an organization's attitudes and actions toward employees or clients (Ouchi 1981;

Pascale and Athos 1981); (5) rules for getting along in the organization (Schein 1968; Van Maanen 1979); and (6) the feeling or organizational climate and the manner in which members of the culture interact with those outside the culture (Tagiuri and Litwin 1968).

Behavioral regularities should not be overemphasized as a manifestation of culture (Schein 1985). Who talks with whom may be more a function of environmental contingencies, such as physical proximity, rather than a behavioral manifestation of deeper assumptions and beliefs at the "core" of culture. For example, inferring cultural groupings based on the location of faculty offices may or may not be appropriate. Faculty with adjoining offices could share cultural bonds—or the arrangement might merely reflect a confluence of factors, such as random space assignment following renovation of the physical plant or historical accident.

The "small homogenous society" analogue used in anthropological studies of culture (discussed later) is sorely strained when applied to many contemporary institutions of higher education. Large public, multipurpose universities are comprised of many different groups whose members may or may not share or abide by all of the institution's norms, values, practices, beliefs, and meanings. Instead of viewing colleges and universities as monolithic entities (Martin and Siehl 1983), it is more realistic to analyze them as multicultural contexts (March and Simon 1958; Van Maanen and Barley 1984) that are host to numerous subgroups with different priorities, traditions, and values (Gregory 1983).

Culture is potentially divisive. If routine patterns of behavior within one group are considered normal, different activities performed by another subgroup may be judged abnormal (Morgan 1986, p. 120). Such ethnocentric behavior may be a form of cultural nearsightedness (Broom and Selznick 1973) or socialized differences that increase the possibility that misunderstandings and conflicts will occur (Gregory 1983).

Faculty in the humanities are socialized into "a structure of values, attitudes, and ways of thinking and feeling" (Clark and Corcoran 1986, p. 30) quite different from the structure to which physicists and chemists are socialized. Career path patterns of faculty in "pure" disciplines (e.g., biology, history) and "applied" fields (e.g., engineering, education) are different. Faculty in the former group learn how to behave by working side by side with senior professors in the laboratory as postdoctoral research associates. Faculty in the latter group are more likely to learn about the academic profession "on the job" during the first years of a professorial appointment after postdoctoral experience as a practicing professional in private industry, government, medicine, law, or education (Becher 1984). These and other differences (epistemological and ideological views, for example) encourage the formation of separate academic clans or subcultures, a topic examined in more depth later.

So how, then, does one define culture? Three and one-half decades ago, Kroeber and Kluckhohn (1952) reported 164 different definitions of culture. Given the myriad qualities contained in the concept of culture, it is not surprising that a common definition remains elusive (Smircich 1983), but it has been defined, for example, as:

> *The core set of assumptions, understandings, and implicit rules that govern day-to-day behavior in the workplace* (Deal and Kennedy 1983, p. 498);

> *The shared philosophies, ideologies, values, assumptions, beliefs, expectations, attitudes, and norms that knit a community together* (Kilmann et al. 1985, p. 5);

> *The traditional and social heritage of a people; their customs and practices; their transmitted knowledge, beliefs, law, and morals; their linguistic and symbolic forms of communication, and the meanings they share* (Becher 1984, p. 167);

> *An interpretive paradigm...both a product and process, the shaper of human interaction and the outcome of it, continually created and recreated by people's ongoing interactions* (Jelinek, Smircich, and Hirsch 1983, p. 331).

Based on a review of the literature, another definition of culture is "the shared values, assumptions, beliefs, or ideologies that participants have about their organization (colleges and universities)" (Peterson et al. 1986, p. 81). While this definition is parsimonious, it does not explicitly acknowledge the influence culture has on the behavior of faculty and students, the holistic, evolutionary qualities of culture, and the influence of the external environment on institutional culture.

For the purposes of this report, then, culture in higher education is defined as *the collective, mutually shaping patterns of norms, values, practices, beliefs, and assumptions that guide the behavior of individuals and groups in an institute of higher education and provide a frame of reference within which to interpret the meaning of events and actions on and off campus.* This definition emphasizes normative influences on behavior as well as the underlying system of assumptions and beliefs shared by culture bearers.

Properties of Culture

This section describes many of the subtle aspects of experience subsumed under the concept of culture as a complex whole, paying particular attention to artifactual manifestations of culture as they can be observed and providing clues to hidden properties (e.g., values and assumptions).

Culture and meaning are inextricably intertwined (Hall 1976).

> *The more we have learned about colleges, the more we have been struck by their uniqueness. True, colleges run to "types," and types ultimately converge on a national academic model. One might therefore lump together the Universities of Massachusetts and Connecticut, or Harvard and Yale, or Boston College and Fordham, or San Francisco State and San Diego. But on closer inspection these colleges appear to draw on quite different publics and to have quite different flavors* (Riesman and Jencks 1962, p. 132).

Because culture is bound to a context, every institution's culture is different. Therefore, the meaning of behavior can be interpreted only through a real-life situation within a specific college's cultural milieu (Hall 1976). To attempt to divorce an interpretation of behavior "from what happens—at this time or in that place, what specific people say, what they do, what is done to them, from the whole vast business of the world—is to divorce it from its applications and render it vacant" (Geertz 1973, p. 18). Thus, descriptions and interpretations of events and actions from one institution are not generalizable to other institutions. "The essential task [is] not to generalize across cases but to generalize within them" (Geertz 1973, p. 20).

The manner in which culture is transmitted and through which individuals derive meaning from their experiences within the cultural milieu are essentially tacit (Geertz 1973; Hall 1976; Schein 1985). In this sense, culture is an "unconscious infrastructure" (Smircich 1983), a paradigm for understanding nuances of behavior shaped by shared understandings, assump-

tions, and beliefs. The cultural paradigm serves as an organizing framework within which to determine rewards and punishments, what is valued and what is not, and moral imperatives (see, for example, Gardner 1986; Schein 1985) that bond individuals and groups and order behavior. Culture provides contextual clues (Hall 1976) necessary to interpret behaviors, words, and acts and gives these actions and events meaning within the culture bearers' frame of reference (Corbett, Firestone, and Rossman 1987). Culture also enhances stability in a college or university through the socialization of new members (Van Maanen and Barley 1984). Because culture exists largely below the level of conscious thought and because culture bearers may themselves disagree on the meaning of artifacts and other properties of culture, describing the culture of a college or university in a way that all faculty and students find satisfactory may not be possible (Allaire and Firsirotu 1984).

> *[Culture is] a process of reality construction that allows people to see and understand particular events, actions, objects, utterances, or situations in distinctive ways. These patterns of understanding also provide a basis for making one's own behavior sensible and meaningful.... [Culture is] an active living phenomenon through which people create and recreate the worlds in which they live* (Morgan 1986, pp. 128, 131).

Thus, although culture is fairly stable, it is always evolving, continually created and recreated by ongoing patterns of interactions between individuals, groups, and an institution's internal and external environments. Although these patterns of interaction may change over time to reflect changing assumptions, values, and preferences, they are stable enough to define and shape what is acknowledged to be appropriate behavior in a particular setting. Thus, the dominant constellation of assumptions, values, and preferences introduces and socializes new members into the accepted patterns of behavior, thereby perpetuating—for all practical purposes—many of the dominant assumptions and beliefs of the culture. In this sense, culture provides stability for a college during turbulent periods and also contributes to the general effectiveness of the institution (Smircich 1983) by reminding students and faculty of what the institution values and by punishing undesirable behavior.

The press toward behaving in culturally acceptable ways, which is invariably an outcome of a strong culture (Deal and

Kennedy 1982; Gregory 1983), may constrain innovation or attempts to do things differently. A dominant culture presents difficulties to newcomers or members of underrepresented groups when trying to understand and appreciate the nuances of behavior. At worst, culture can be an alienating, ethnocentric force that goads members of a group, sometimes out of fear and sometimes out of ignorance, to reinforce their own beliefs while rejecting those of other groups (Gregory 1983).

The relative strength of a culture or subculture is impossible to determine (Van Maanen and Barley 1984). While this question begs for an empirical answer, the weight of the argument seems to be on the side of those who claim that cultures do vary in the degree to which they influence members' behavior and guide institutional responses in times of crisis (Deal and Kennedy 1982; Peters and Waterman 1982).

Some writers have developed typologies or inventories of organizational characteristics based on their observations of what seem to be "healthy" cultures (see, for example, Peters and Waterman 1982; Peterson et al. 1986). Given the context-bound, perspectival qualities of culture, however, attempts to determine whether one institutional culture is better than another seem wrongheaded. Some institutional cultures clearly support research activity over undergraduate instruction and vice versa (Riesman and Jencks 1962). University trustees, state legislators, and students will continue to be wary of prevailing norms that encourage faculty to cloister themselves in library carrels or in the research laboratory rather than increase the number of office hours to meet with students. Standards for academic productivity, such as papers published or number of courses and students taught, are different in a church-related liberal arts college, a state-supported university whose mission is teacher education, and a research-oriented university (Austin and Gamson 1983; Baldridge et al. 1977).

Any culture has two basic components: (1) "substance, or the networks of meanings contained in its ideologies, norms, and values; and (2) forms, or the practices whereby these meanings are expressed, affirmed, and communicated to members" (Trice and Beyer 1984, p. 654). In this sense, culture is both a product and a process.

Culture has been discussed as both an independent and a dependent variable (Ouchi and Wilkins 1985; Peterson et al. 1986). Culture, when viewed as an independent variable, is a complex, continually evolving web of assumptions, beliefs, symbols, and interactions carried by faculty, students, and other culture bearers (Smircich 1983) that cannot be directly purposefully controlled by any person or group. Culture as a dependent variable is the constellation of shared values and beliefs manifested through patterns of behavior like rituals, ideologies, and patterns of interactions. An administrator may attempt to change seemingly dysfunctional aspects of a culture by encouraging different behaviors on the part of faculty and students, and suggestions have been offered about how one might attempt to manipulate organizational culture (Kilmann et al. 1985; Ouchi 1981; Peters and Waterman 1982). The culture of a college or university—as substance and form, as process and product, and as independent and dependent variables—shapes human interactions and reflects the outcomes of mutually shaping interactions (Louis 1980; Siehl and Martin 1982; Smircich 1983).

Levels of Culture
Some find the essence of culture to be the tacit assumptions and beliefs that influence the way a group of people think and behave (Schein 1985). These guiding assumptions and beliefs, which are below the surface of conscious thought, are manifested in observable forms or artifacts. In an effort to increase analytical precision and avoid unnecessary confusion, Schein (1985) divided culture into a conceptual hierarchy comprised of three levels: artifacts, values, and basic assumptions and beliefs.

Artifacts
"Meanings are 'stored' in symbols" (Geertz 1973, p. 127). Because artifacts are largely symbols of culture, they represent a multitude of meanings and emotions. Evidence of an institution's culture may be found in norms, mores, formal and informal rules, routine procedures, behaviors that are rewarded or punished, customs, folkways, myths, daily and periodic rituals, ceremonies, interaction patterns, signs, and a language system common to the culture bearers (Broom and Selznick 1973; Morgan 1986; Schein 1985; Tierney 1985, 1987; Van Maanen and Barley 1984). A rite combines discrete cultural forms into an integrated, unified public performance. A ceremonial is the linking of several rites into a single occasion or event (Chapple and Coon 1942). For example, most commencement ceremonies are made up of discrete rites: the formation of candidates

for degrees into one or more lines, the procession of faculty and students, the commencement address, the conferral of honorary degrees, the conferral of various degrees (baccalaureate, master's, professional school, Ph.D.), the hooding of doctoral degree recipients, the alumni association's welcome to those receiving degrees, the tossing of mortarboards into the air at the conclusion of the formal event, and the recession from the site of commencement.

Table 1 (page 18) defines other frequently mentioned cultural forms (see also Boje, Fedor, and Rowland 1982). To underscore the connectedness and cumulative contributions of what appear to be discrete artifacts to the "whole" of culture, ritual, language, stories, and myths are discussed in some detail.

Rituals communicate meaning within a college community by calling attention to and transmitting important values, welcoming and initiating new members (Gardner 1986), and celebrating members' accomplishments. Essentially a social construction, rituals—such as convocations, graduations, presidential inaugurations, activities of secret societies, and dedications (Bushnell 1962)—help to create, maintain, and invent "patterns of collective action and social structure" (Burns 1978, p. 265; see also Turner and Turner 1985). "Above all, rituals are dramas of persuasion. They are didactic, enacted pronouncements concerning the meaning of an occasion and the nature and worth of the people involved in the occasion" (Myerhoff 1977, p. 22). Thus, rituals make statements about the quality of life within the community and set standards against which people are asked to compare and modify behavior, values, activities, and relationships (Manning 1987).

Rituals are staged, public, and stylized versions of how things should be and beliefs about how things are that eloquently describe and shape cultural patterns (Goody 1977). Although the possibilities for expression are endless, similar patterns are repeated over time and become part of, as well as reflect, a group's history. These patterns teach cooperation, the importance of tradition, social relations and solidarity, tasks and goals of the group, and the place of authority (Burns and Laughlin 1979; Moore and Myerhoff 1977).

Rituals have certain properties:

1. A collective dimension in which the social meaning inherent in the community is expressed

TABLE 1
DEFINITIONS OF FREQUENTLY STUDIED CULTURAL FORMS

Rite	Relatively elaborate, dramatic, planned sets of activities that consolidate various forms of cultural expressions into one event (e.g., dissertation defense meeting); carried out through social interactions, usually for the benefit of an audience.
Ceremonial	A system of several rites connected with a single occasion or event (e.g., commencement, orientation).
Ritual	A standardized, detailed set of techniques and behaviors that manage anxieties but seldom produce intended technical consequences of practical importance (e.g., freshman induction convocation, required chapel).
Myth	A dramatic narrative of imagined events, usually used to explain origins or transformations of something; also, an unquestioned belief about the practical benefits of certain techniques and behaviors that is not supported by demonstrated facts.
Saga	A historical narrative describing the unique accomplishments of a group and its leaders, usually in heroic terms (see Clark 1972).

2. Repetition in content, form, and occasion
3. Self-conscious or deliberate action by the participants as part of the special behavior or stylized performance
4. Orderly action achieved through exaggerated precision and
5. Evocative style of presentation and staging to engage and focus the attention of the audience (Manning 1987; Myerhoff 1977).

Rituals depend on a system of *language* to communicate important ideas and feelings (Gordon 1969). Language is more than an inventory of words and expressions to describe objects and behaviors; it is a guide to social reality that typifies, stabilizes, and integrates experience into a meaningful whole (Petti-

Legend	A handed-down narrative of some wonderful event that is based in history but has been embellished with fictional details.
Story	A narrative based on true events, often a combination of truth and fiction.
Folktale	A completely fictional narrative.
Symbol	Any object, act, event, quality, or relation that serves as a vehicle for conveying meaning, usually by representing another thing (e.g., school mascot, campus statues, or other objects, such as the axe that symbolizes rivalry between the University of California at Berkeley and Stanford—Basu 1984).
Language	A particular form or manner in which members of a group use vocal sounds and written signs to convey meanings to each other (e.g., an institution's fight song or Alma Mater).
Gesture	Movements of parts of the body used to express meanings.
Physical setting	Those things that surround people physically and provide them with immediate sensory stimuli as they carry out culturally expressive activities.
Artifact	Material objects manufactured by people to facilitate culturally expressive activities.

Source: Adapted from Trice (1984) and Trice and Beyer (1984).

grew 1979). All cultures have a language that links "the collective, cultural, and cognitive domains" of everyday living (Forgas 1985, p. 252). Language systems are based on symbols and metaphors and serve as analogues of life that convey thoughts, perceptions, and feelings associated with experiences in a particular social context (Bredeson 1987; Langer 1953). "Language is not (as commonly thought) a system for transferring thoughts or meaning...but a system for organizing information and releasing thoughts and responses in other organisms" (Hall 1976, p. 49). Thus, symbols and metaphors do not so much reflect reality as translate it in a form that can be shared and understood by others (Morgan, Frost, and Pondy 1983). Because colleges and universities are rich in symbolism and ceremony, an awareness of the systems of symbols that mediate meaning between individuals and their cultures is important to understanding events and actions (Kuh, Whitt, and Shedd 1987; Masland 1985).

Symbols, such as organizational signs, communicate the value placed on time, space, and communication, different modes by which institutional agents express their feelings about others, and the activities of a college.

Signs exist as fluid examples of how people define and give meaning to organizational culture. Thus, signs change over time and acquire and lose power due to the constantly shifting nature of the organization and its participants (Tierney 1987, pp. 20–21).

The significance of analyzing how leaders spend their time, where they spend it, and how they communicate (writing, speaking from written notes) leads to different understandings about how people within a college may influence organizational leadership and decision making. For example, how faculty members or administrators spend time can be effective at one university and inefficient elsewhere because of the cultural meaning given to time in their institutional context (Tierney 1985). Organizational time has three different dimensions: formal/informal, historical, and seasonal/ceremonial (Tierney 1985). The formal and informal use of time refers to how individuals structure their own time, such as appointments and meetings, versus dropping in for a visit (Deal and Kennedy 1982; Peters and Waterman 1982).

Historical time refers to the manner in which individuals and organizations use the experience of the past in responding to current challenges (Gadamer 1979), while seasonal or ceremonial time refers to the institutional events with which people attempt to synchronize their own activities. Seasonal festivals, the beginning and ending of academic years, the informal coffee hour, the preregistration period, the change in athletic seasons, the movement from outdoors to indoors in the winter and vice versa in the spring all impart organizational meaning and have an influence on how faculty and students perceive and act in a college or university. Problems can arise when administrators rely on a functional interpretation of time that violates the institution's conception of ceremonial time.

At one institution,...Honors Day and Founders Day tradi-
tionally were in the fall. A new president and a new aca-
demic vice president decided to delay the ceremonies until
springtime. They had proposed a massive overhaul of the ac-
ademic and fiscal sides of the institution, and they did not
believe they had time to spend on Honors Day or Founders
Day....

The community decried the move. One observer noted,
"It's kind of chintzy if you ask me. It used to be really spe-
cial and everything." Another person said, "Those days
stand for what we're about. Everybody got involved, and in
one fell swoop they just decided to get rid of them, tell us
that we've got to stick to our desks" (Tierney 1985, p. 17).

How time is used influences sense making. What is appropriate
use of time in one institutional culture may be inappropriate at
another (Tierney 1985).

Stories are narratives—complete with plots, protagonists, an-
tagonists, and action—that shape other aspects of the institutional culture, such as behavioral norms. Stories serve at least
five functions: (1) providing information about rules in the institution or subculture; (2) reflecting the beliefs that faculty,
students, and alumni have about how past events occurred,
thereby keeping the institutional memory sharp (Wilkins 1983);
(3) increasing commitment and loyalty to the institution; (4)
undergirding and reinforcing other artifacts of culture; and (5)
connecting current faculty and students with the institution's
past and present (Brown, cited in Kelly 1985). Although stories
provide distinctive information about a college, certain characteristics of stories are similar at many institutions (Martin et al.
1983). For example, written histories of colleges often describe
the founders of the institution as heroes and depict, in sagalike
language, the trials and travails endured in establishing the college (Clark 1970, 1972).

As stories are passed from one student generation to another
(Trippet 1982), the stories sometimes take on legendary proportions and become tightly woven into the fabric of the institutional culture. Stories are told at Wabash College in Indiana
about the founders of the college kneeling in the snow watch-
ing the burning of South Hall, the marching off to war of the
"entire" student body in the 1860s, and the bloody class fights
on Washington's birthday. Such stories, perpetuated by faculty
members and administrators alike, sometimes have more influ-

Such stories, perpetuated by faculty members and administrators alike, sometimes have more influence on decisions and institutional commitments than policies or data from management information systems.

ence on decisions and institutional commitments than policies or data from management information systems (Martin and Powers 1983).

Myths are substantially fictional narratives of events, usually expressed in symbolic terms and often endowed with an almost sacred quality (Allaire and Firsirotu 1984; Cohen 1969). Myths develop over time "to mediate and otherwise 'manage' basic organizational dilemmas," such as ambiguity and uncertainty (Boje, Fedor, and Rowland 1982, p. 27). Myths perform five functions: (1) legitimizing and rationalizing intended or completed actions and consequences; (2) mediating between political interests and competing values; (3) explaining or creating causal relationships; (4) dealing with turbulence in the external environment through rationalization; and (5) enriching the life of the institution or group (Boje, Fedor, and Rowland 1982). An innovative campus, the University of California–Santa Cruz attracted students with liberal social attitudes and developed the reputation for being "flaky" and "touchy-feely." A mythical tale about the origins of the school circulated among students during the 1960s:

> *Like other conspiracy theories of the sixties, the myth was laced with paranoia and hysteria. The central administration of the University of California, the story went, had planned the Santa Cruz campus as a home for radical students. Like some enormous Venus's fly trap, innovation would attract the unorthodox. But the rural setting, decentralized structure, and close student-faculty contact envisioned for Santa Cruz would effectively disarm radical criticism of the university, turning potentially angry humanists into compliant and hard-working students* (Adams 1984, pp. 21–22).

As with many myths, a kernel of truth was imbedded in this example. In the 1950s, predating student activism by about a decade, Clark Kerr, then president of the University of California system, and Dean McHenry, Kerr's assistant for academic planning (who later became chancellor of the Santa Cruz campus), envisioned the need for a campus that would be committed to innovative undergraduate education (Grant and Riesman 1978). Kerr and McHenry had no interest in isolating radicals; they were, however, committed to minimizing the bureaucracy of the research-oriented university in an effort to personalize the experience at Santa Cruz (Adams 1984).

Sometimes additional insights into culture can be gleaned from an analysis of organizational structure (Clark and Trow 1966) and substantive products like policy statements and standard operating procedures. Structure, as represented by an organizational chart, provides a point of reference for the way people think about and make sense of the contexts in which they work (Deal and Kennedy 1982). Written statements of institutional philosophy, mission, and purpose may communicate important messages to faculty, students, and others about what is valued in the institution. Artifacts also may take the form of technologies, such as ways of organizing work, how decisions are made, and course reservation and registration procedures for students (Kuh, Whitt, and Shedd 1987).

Identifying artifacts is relatively easy. It is much more difficult to determine how the nested patterns of assumptions and beliefs represented by artifacts influence the behavior of individuals and groups across time (Schein 1985). Slogans, symbols, language patterns, stories, myths, ceremonials, and rituals provide clues to a deeper, pervasive system of meaning. To understand the culture of a college or university is "to understand how this system, in its mundane as well as its more dramatic aspects, is created and sustained" (Morgan 1986, p. 133). Such understanding can be acquired by linking or contrasting artifacts with the values used in decision making (Schein 1985).

Values

The second level of culture (Schein 1985) is made up of values—widely held beliefs or sentiments about the importance of certain goals, activities, relationships, and feelings. Four values influence the academic enterprise: justice, competence, liberty, and loyalty (Clark 1984). Some institutional values are conscious and explicitly articulated; they serve a normative or moral function by guiding members' responses to situations. Most institutional values, however, are unconsciously expressed as themes (e.g., academic freedom, tradition of collegial governance) or are symbolic interpretations of reality that give meaning to social actions and establish standards for social behavior (Clark and Trow 1966). They often take the form of context-bound values that are related directly to a college's vitality and well-being (Clark 1970; Riesman and Jencks 1962; Sanford 1967).

In *The Small Room* (Sarton 1961), the faculty of a selective Eastern liberal arts college face a dilemma: The institution's lit-

erary journal published a promising student's paper that contained plagiarized material. The appropriate institutional response is problematic because the faculty feel they may have placed an undue amount of pressure on the student to perform brilliantly. The discussion among several faculty directly involved in the matter reveals the tension between the values of academic integrity, honesty, intellectual achievement, and the student's social-emotional well-being:

> "Well," Lucy swallowed and paused, then began in a rather stiff cold voice, "I think I am clear that Jane was put under more stress than she could stand. It looks to me as if she broke down not after the affair exploded, but that the real breakdown was clear in the act itself of stealing the Weil essay, and that she did it as a way out of unbearable pressure"....
>
> "You suggest that Professor Cope asked too much out of Jane?"....
>
> "Do you feel that there is an overemphasis on intellectual achievement in the college as a whole? Is that the essence?"
>
> "...If Lucy is right...then a serious attack is being made on the values of this college. We are going to have to do some hard thinking"....
>
> "...With your permission, I am going to call the faculty [together] and present Jane's case in light of all we have been saying. I shall try to move away from the passions all this has aroused to the big questions that confront us..."
> (pp. 179–81).

Cultural values are likely to be tightly linked to, or at least congruent with, basic beliefs and assumptions (the deepest level of culture, to be discussed next) and are embodied in the institution's philosophy or ideology, a "relatively coherent set of beliefs that bind some people together and that explain their worlds [to them] in terms of cause-and-effect relations" (Beyer 1981, p. 166). In this sense, values provide the basis for a system of beliefs (Allaire and Firsirotu 1984).

An illustration of using institutional values to work through dilemmas is provided in a description of Ryke College (a pseudonym), an urban, midwestern Protestant liberal arts college (1,635 full-time equivalent students) founded in 1874 that—like many institutions in the 1970s—was confronted with financial troubles precipitated by declining enrollments (Chaffee 1983).

Three major traditions characterized Ryke's history: (1) a mutually supportive relationship with and commitment to its urban setting, (2) an openness to international perspectives, and (3) involvement in social causes. Although Ryke's faculty were receptive to new curricular ideas, any changes were cautiously integrated into the existing classical liberal arts curriculum. The strategy Ryke College followed was to hold fast to the image of "a small, fine liberal arts college" (Chaffee 1983, p. 182).

Ryke's values served as a bridge between artifacts and basic assumptions and beliefs. Ryke's new president attempted to make the college visible again within the urban community. The faculty renewed their commitment to a core liberal arts curriculum consistent with the institution's original mission. The college also made certain its mission statement and recruitment and socialization practices for faculty and students were consistent with the guiding values of the institution. Apparently, the key to the survival of this institution was "being true to its historical liberal arts mission..." (Chaffee 1983, p. 183).

Values sometimes surface as exhortations about what is right or wrong, what is encouraged or discouraged—what "ought" to be. For example, statements by the chief academic officer about the importance of teaching or by the chief student life officer about the debilitating consequences of the inappropriate use of alcohol can, under certain circumstances (e.g., when the statements are repeated often and are accompanied by behavior suggesting the authenticity of the statements), communicate the institution's values. Of course, some values are merely espoused (Argyris and Schon 1978) and predict what people will say in certain situations but may not represent what they do. Espoused values are more like aspirations or rationalizations (Schein 1985). Examples of espoused values abound in many colleges and universities: commitment to increasing minority representation in the student body and faculty, assertions about the importance of undergraduate instruction in research universities, and mission statements underscoring an institution's commitment to students' holistic development.

Basic assumptions and beliefs
The third level, believed to be the core of culture, consists of basic but often unstated assumptions that undergird artifacts and values (Schein 1985). These assumptions and beliefs are learned responses to threats to institutional survival and exert a powerful influence over what people think about, what they

perceive to be important, how they feel about things, and what they do (Schein 1985). Indeed, assumptions and beliefs determine the way reality is perceived and (albeit unconsciously) guide behavior. These conceptions are so deeply ingrained that they are by definition taken for granted, "not confrontable or debatable" (Schein 1985, p. 18); thus, such assumptions are difficult to identify.

The difficulty in identifying assumptions and beliefs is acknowledged in the advocacy of the use of a culture audit to systematically review aspects of an organization that reflect culture (Wilkins 1983). Tacit assumptions and beliefs are not possible to articulate. Assumptions may be implied, however, through concrete examples. ("I can't explain it in so many words, but I can give you a lot of examples"—Wilkins 1983, p. 27). Thus, to discover distinctive patterns of beliefs and assumptions, one must sift through numerous, diverse artifacts and talk with students and faculty at great length.

The existence of subcultures also adds to the challenge of mapping core assumptions. Clashes of subcultures may point to conflicting core assumptions (Wilkins 1983), such as students' expectation that the institution should prepare them for a vocation, while faculty assume the institution should provide adequate resources for them to pursue scholarly interests. Faculty expect that collegial governance structures can and should be used to guide the direction of the institution, while administrators, under pressure to make decisions and allocate resources, behave in what may appear to faculty to be a unilateral, rigidly bureaucratic manner.

Summary

Culture is a complex set of context-bound, continually evolving properties that potentially includes anything influencing events and actions in a college or university (Tierney 1988). As a result, precise definitions of culture remain elusive. Rituals, stories, language, and other artifacts are observable manifestations of culture that reflect deeper values and help faculty, students, staff, alumni, and others understand what is appropriate and important under certain situations. The core of culture is comprised of assumptions and beliefs shared—to some degree—by members of the institution that guide decision making and shape major events and activities.

Colleges and universities are not monolithic entities. Subgroups have their own artifacts and values, which may differ from the host's institutional culture. The next section reviews the disciplinary perspectives that have been used to study cultural phenomena.

INTELLECTUAL FOUNDATIONS OF CULTURE

Many fields have contributed to contemporary connotations of the concept of culture, including psychology, semiotics, communications, and social psychology. Current conceptions of culture have emerged primarily from two disciplines, however—anthropology and sociology (Ouchi and Wilkins 1985; Peterson et al. 1986), the intellectual foundations of culture summarized in this section. The following brief overviews of anthropology and sociology are admittedly simplified and rely heavily on Allaire and Firsirotu's excellent summary (1984) of the contributions of anthropology to culture and the insights into the sociology of culture provided by Ouchi and Wilkins (1985) and Van Maanen and Barley (1984).

By legitimating and emphasizing the "hidden," phenomenological, nonrational aspects of culture . . . cultural anthropology makes important contributions to understanding culture in colleges and universities.

Anthropology

Anthropology has been defined as "the science of man and culture" (Hoebel 1966, p. 4) and is generally divided into two major subdivisions: (1) physical anthropology—the study of biological characteristics of ancient and modern human populations; and (2) cultural anthropology—the study of the customs, beliefs, folkways, and behaviors characteristic of human societies (Hoebel 1966), which is further subdivided into ethnography, ethnology, social anthropology, and linguistics, among other fields.

Anthropological approaches to culture have been influenced by Tylor's definition of culture: "that complex whole [that] includes knowledge, belief, art, law, morals, custom, and any other capability and habits acquired by man as a member of society" (cited in Kroeber and Kluckhohn 1952, p. 81). Anthropologists have focused on basic social units of primitive societies, such as hunting and gathering bands or residents of small villages (Allaire and Firsirotu 1984; Hoebel 1966). The differences between primitive societies and complex social organizations, such as the modern American university, are arguably so great that the contributions of anthropological approaches to culture may be misleading (Erickson 1987). By legitimating and emphasizing the "hidden," phenomenological, nonrational aspects of culture (Hall 1976) that are currently receiving attention in the higher education literature (Peterson et al. 1986), cultural anthropology makes important contributions to understanding culture in colleges and universities. According to Allaire and Firsirotu (1984), two traditions are prominent within cultural anthropology: the sociocultural and the ideational.

Sociocultural tradition

Until the 1960s, sociocultural views of culture dominated anthropology. This tradition holds that social systems arise and are maintained through personal interactions that produce common expectations and understandings. Behaviors that create bonds of shared experience are emphasized. A system of shared beliefs is considered an integral aspect of culture that, along with other socially constructed roles and institutions (e.g., families or kinship roots), shapes or defines appropriate behavior. The sociocultural tradition includes five contrasting perspectives: functionalism, structural-functionalism, ecological-adaptationism, historical-diffusionism, and cultural materialism (Allaire and Firsirotu 1984; Harris 1968).

Functionalism. Culture is instrumental in that it helps people cope with concrete problems encountered in everyday life (Malinowski 1961). Organizational structures evolve over time in response to members' interests. For example, the emergence of an organizational saga (Clark 1972), stories, and myths can be viewed as functional because they satisfy basic needs for affiliation, security, order, and understanding.

Structural-functionalism. In this view, culture is an adaptive mechanism by which a group of persons becomes an ordered community and shares a social life in a particular setting (Radcliffe-Brown 1952). Culture is a major aspect of a social system that also includes a formal social structure that delineates status and roles within the group. The formal social structure cannot be discontinuous or disjunctive with the host culture; therefore, the formal organizational structure of a college or university can be expected to be consistent with the institution's values. This point of view is sometimes called "synchronic" (e.g., language and behavior are in sync and are culturally bound—Allaire and Firsirotu 1984; Hall 1976); culture can be understood only at a particular time and place in the context of a specific problem. Thus, the function of culture is to maintain the social system, in the form of relationships between individuals and groups, and to adapt the system to constraints and opportunities in the surrounding environment.

Ecological-adaptationism. Culture is a system of socially transmitted behavior patterns that connect human communities to their settings. As a human system, a college is in a mutual, shaping relationship with its environment. Neither the institution's culture nor the environment can be defined independent of the other; each influences the development of the other. The values of an organization may differ significantly from those of the host society and become a subculture (Sanford 1962a); however, in this view, as in the structural-functionalist view, the institution's values are generally consistent with its social structure.

Historical-diffusionism. This view holds that cultural forms are shaped by historical circumstances and evolve through a process of acculturation and assimilation. Some elements of one culture may "migrate" to other cultures through individuals' interactions with persons from other cultures. The issues and concerns prominent at the time of the founding of a college may be represented in strongly held values and ideologies that continue to influence organizational structures and processes (Clark 1970). The ecological-adaptationist and the historical-diffusionist views are considered diachronic (e.g., they emphasize changes in language and behavior patterns across time) and focus on the development of particular cultures at different times in history (Allaire and Firsirotu 1984; Hall 1976).

Cultural materialism. Cultural materialism is based on the Marxist principle that the modes of material production in a society determine the character of social, economic, political, and spiritual processes; it offers a different view of how cultures evolve over time (Harris 1968). At the root of cultural materialism is the assumption that human collectives face common threats to their existence (e.g., production of goods, reproduction, and maintaining the social order). People rely on cultural mechanisms to cope with these problems (Harris 1979). Thus, means of production (e.g., technology, work patterns) and reproduction (e.g., mating patterns, forms of nurturance, contraception) work together to establish a political economy (e.g., governance structures, educational institutions, police) and a domestic economy (e.g., family structures, age and sex roles). The evolution of a culture can be described by tracking changes in myths, ideologies, religion, symbols, taboos, and kinship systems common to political and domestic economies.

Cultural materialism has also been described as a "scientific research strategy" (Harris 1979, p. 5), because cultural phenomena are defined from an etic (an external observer's) rather than an emic (internal, personal) point of view. Thus, in the study of cultural properties, external processes (e.g., technology) are emphasized over internal processes (e.g., sense making).

Ideational

In the past 25 years, the ideational tradition has become a prominent anthropological view of culture. Proponents of this tradition believe that language and symbols are the primary vehicles through which people apprehend or make meaning of their experience (Geertz 1973; Ouchi and Wilkins 1985; Peterson et al. 1986). "The whole point of [an ideational] approach to culture is to aid us in gaining access to the conceptual world in which our subjects live so that we can, in some extended sense of the term, converse with them" (Geertz 1973, p. 24). This tradition has four distinct perspectives: cognitive or ethnographic, structuralist, mutual equivalence, and symbolic or semiotic (Allaire and Firsirotu 1984).

Cognitive or ethnographic. In this view, culture is a system of knowledge or a set of learned standards for perceiving, believing, evaluating, and acting. Culture is a "unique system for perceiving and organizing material phenomena, things, events, behavior, and emotions" (Goodenough, cited in Rossi and Higgins 1980, p. 63). Those interested in learning about culture from a cognitive view attempt to discover, by analyzing social interactions, the rules for perceiving and organizing (Smircich 1983). This position is compatible with Argyris and Schon's description (1978) of organizations as cognitive enterprises and the role of a paradigm in scientific communities. Both represent organized patterns of thinking or world views that lead to understanding of what constitutes adequate knowledge and legitimate activity (Smircich 1983).

Structuralist. In another view, culture is made up of systems of symbols that are cumulative products of mind; the products reflect unconscious processes and predilections (Levi-Strauss 1973). "Universals" or general laws make up a psychodynamic structure that enables members of groups to understand behavior within their particular social settings. These universals influence how organizational forms and structures come about; that is, "the basic features of the organization's structure and function derive from the characteristics of human problem-solving processes and rational human choice" (March and Simon 1958, p. 169). Another example of using a structuralist approach to penetrate beneath the surface of organizational events and actions is the application of Jung's archetypes to understand differences in the behavior of managers (Mitroff 1983a). People are thought to have a distinctive framework or underlying structure by which they organize and give meaning to events and actions around them (Morgan, Frost, and Pondy 1983; Taylor 1984). An archetype is an unconscious predisposition to consistently use a particular system of beliefs to make sense of experience. As with a scientific paradigm, archetypal behavior provides predictable responses in complex situations; at the same time, the available courses of action are constrained for an administrator whose behavior is archetypal.

Mutual equivalence. In this view, culture is a set of standardized cognitions making up a general framework for predicting and understanding behavior within the context of a social setting. Through repeated interactions, tacit understandings gradually emerge over time, allowing individuals to work together more effectively to attain personal and collective goals (Wallace 1970). In this sense, a college or university becomes a convenient vehicle through which faculty and students can pursue their varied interests and goals. "This view of 'culture' is almost opposite to the conventional meaning...with its evocation of 'shared values, beliefs, and norms' " (Allaire and Firsirotu 1984, p. 206). The mutual-equivalence view is compatible with the conception of organizations as settings that allow participants to exchange incentives (Georgiou 1973) and the thesis that collective structures result from repetitive, mutually reinforcing behavioral loops (Weick 1979). Both views suggest that organizations exist not to pursue common goals but to permit individuals to attain personal goals.

Symbolic or semiotic. In the first three ideational views, culture is created in the minds of the culture bearers. In this view, culture does not live in people's heads but emerges through shared meanings conveyed by symbols and signs and becomes a "fabric of meaning in terms of which human beings interpret their experience and guide their action" (Geertz 1973, p. 145). In this sense, events and actions in a college or university "have no external reality but are merely social creations and constructions *emerging* from actors making sense out of ongoing streams of actions and interactions" (Allaire and Firsirotu 1984, p. 208; see also Berger and Luckmann 1966 and Burrell and Morgan 1979). Thus, in the symbolic perspective, culture is an interpretative mechanism brought to life by an individual's attempt to make meaning of his or her relationship with the external environment—an individual's *Umwelt*. *Umwelt*, a term coined by the German ethnologist Jacob Von Uxkull, differs from traditional views of cognition that equate the environment with a physical setting that shapes or stimulates behavior. The environment, therefore, is not independent of a person but exists only in relation to an individual (Cunningham 1984).

In a famous example, Von Uxkull...described the various Umwelts *created by a tree: a rough textured and convoluted terrain for a bug, a menacing form for a young child, a set of limbs for a nesting bird, and so on. In all these cases, the environment of the tree was the same; that is, the bark, the height, the limbs were "available" to each of the organisms, yet their experience of them was quite different* (Cunningham 1984, p. 416).

To understand events and actions in a college or university, one must appreciate how faculty and students interpret those events and actions and how their interpretations lead to action and the meaning given to action in the college setting.

The sociocultural and ideational traditions can be distinguished in two ways (Peterson et al. 1986): (1) whose point of view is considered "legitimate"—the ostensibly objective researcher observing individual acts within the context of the institution's social system (sociocultural) or the culture as it exists in the minds of or is interpreted by "natives" (ideational) (Gregory 1983); and (2) the level of analysis—institutional/group (sociocultural) or individual culture bearer (ideational). In the sociocultural tradition, culture *does* something; in the ideational tradition, culture *is* something (Peterson et al. 1986).

Summary
Much of the corporate culture literature (cf. Deal and Kennedy 1982; Pascale and Athos 1981; Peters and Waterman 1982) is derived from the sociocultural tradition. Anthropologists identified with the sociocultural tradition, such as Malinowski and Radcliffe-Brown, however, probably would be "appalled by

the explicitly promanagement and change-oriented bias'' (Ouchi and Wilkins 1985, p. 460) advocated in corporate culture models. This approach reduces culture to just another "management tool" similar to the more technical, reductionistic approaches that were faddish in the 1970s (e.g., management by objectives, planning and programmed budgeting systems) (Gregory 1983; Smircich 1983). Whether culture can be manipulated to influence the direction or course of a college or university is debatable, particularly if subcultures, or even countercultures, exist within the institution.

Sociology

Sociology is the study of the basic structure of human society (Broom and Selznick 1973). Sociologists interested in the study of culture have emphasized how divisions of class and race within major societal institutions (e.g., schools and colleges) influence policy, the economy, and the legal system (Bates 1987; Broom and Selznick 1973). The exercise of power and authority is more anonymous in large, complex societies than in the smaller societies typically studied by anthropologists. For this reason and others, an analysis of social structures may be more useful than traditional anthropological conceptions of culture when studying aspects of culture in educational institutions (Erickson 1987).

Some nonrational interpretations of behavior in organizations (organized anarchy, loose coupling) have roots in sociological theories of organizations (Cohen and March 1974; Weick 1979). For example, while Weber (1968) and Toennies (1957) emphasized the diversity inherent in organizational life, they also distinguished between explicit and implicit features of organizations; the formal aspects are considered rational and the latter are thought to be nonrational (Peterson et al. 1986). Durkheim (1933) underscored the importance of myth and ritual to maintaining order in a social structure and suggested that collective life relies on symbolic representations of complex patterns of interactions. Underneath the observable apparatus of job descriptions, titles, and organizational charts "may lurk some universal eminent structure corresponding to the needs structure of the members or, perhaps, of those members more able to influence the nature and shape of the organization" (Allaire and Firsirotu 1984, p. 200).

Four major contributions of sociology are relevant to this discussion: (1) an emphasis on formal organizational structure and environmental conditions that create subgroupings; (2) the concept of subculture; (3) an understanding of socialization processes; and (4) an emphasis on enactment as the process of making meaning through social constructions.

Formal organizational properties

Colleges and universities commonly create work settings consistent with bureaucratic models of organizing by placing faculty and staff in relatively insulated roles marked by position titles and affiliations with specific structural units—the Personnel Department, the School of Business, the College of Arts and Sciences, or the Department of Intercollegiate Athletics, for example. Structuring an institute of higher education into work units, roles, and living units (Clark and Trow 1966; Newcomb 1962) influences who is likely to interact with whom. Differential interactions among faculty, students, and professional staff are shaped by hierarchical arrangements, physical proximity, sharing of common tasks or status, functional demands made on some workers by others, perceptions of the organization's relationship with other units, and even historical accidents (Van Maanen 1984). One result of specialization and differentiation thought to characterize colleges and universities is the formation of subcultures (Clark and Trow 1966; Peterson et al. 1986).

Subcultures

The term "subculture" has been used in a wide variety of situations (Bolton and Kammeyer 1972; Clark and Trow 1966; Katchadourian and Boli 1985; Leemon 1972; Yinger 1970). An attempt to curb indiscriminate use of the term synthesizes common sociological interpretations (e.g., Broom and Selznick 1973) into the following, more precise definition of subculture:

> *A normative-value system held by some group or persons who are in persisting interaction, who transmit the norms and values to newcomers by some communicated process, and who exercise some sort of social control to ensure conformity to the norms. Furthermore, the normative-value system of such a group must differ from the normative-value system of the larger, the parent, or the dominant society* (Bolton and Kammeyer 1972, pp. 381–82).

Institutional subcultures have been defined as subgroups of an institution's members who interact regularly with one another, perceive themselves as a distinct group within the institution, share a commonly defined set of problems, and act on the basis of collective understandings unique to their group (Van Maanen and Barley 1985).

Thus, a subculture is more than a collection of people with similar attitudes or behaviors. Members of a subculture interact persistently with one another over a period of time, they are mutually attracted to one another, they are aware of their common orientation (Feldman and Newcomb 1969; Newcomb et al. 1967), and the possibility of punishment by the group influences their behavior (see Walsh 1973 for a succinct summary of the influence of subcultures on behavior). While certain norms and attitudes are different from those of the host or dominant institutional culture, the group does hold to some values of the dominant culture (Broom and Selznick 1973).

Many uses of the subculture concept violate one or more of these criteria and may lead to misleading conclusions (Bolton and Kammeyer 1972). For example, Clark and Trow's typology (1966) offers no evidence about whether members of any of the four "subcultures" (academic, collegiate, vocational, nonconformist) are in persistent interaction or whether the groups punish members to ensure conformity to norms. Role orientation may be a more accurate concept for describing the categories of student groups presented in Clark and Trow's typology (Bolton and Kammeyer 1972). Role orientation is the tendency to associate with others who are like oneself and to behave in a manner compatible with the group's values and beliefs. In a sense, role orientation is a bridge between personality and formal behavioral expectations in a collegiate setting and may be a more appropriate concept than subculture for categorizing students and, by extension, faculty and other groups.

Subcultures, role orientations, and "social types" (Bolton and Kammeyer 1972) suggest that caution should be exercised in determining whether such groups are legitimate targets of studies incorporating the cultural perspective. That is, for the properties of culture (e.g., shared values and beliefs) to be useful in understanding the behavior of group members, the groups should exhibit the characteristics of subculture as described by Van Maanen and Barley (1985).

Socialization

Socialization is cultural learning, the acquisition of values, knowledge, attitudes, skills, and expectations appropriate to a particular culture (Bess 1978; Corcoran and Clark 1984). As the "mechanism through which the existing consensus structure and communication practices are transferred to new generations of participants" (Etzioni 1975, p. 254), socialization promotes role performance and commitment to organizational goals (Clark and Corcoran 1986; Schein 1985). Culture bearers, such as tenured faculty or returning upper-class students, provide newcomers with information necessary to participate successfully in the life of the institution and to make meaning of new roles, tasks, and experiences (Clark and Corcoran 1986; Van Maanen 1978). Over time, newcomers begin to integrate their own needs and goals with the institution's needs and goals in a manner compatible with norms, values, and roles they perceive to be appropriate and desirable (Bess 1978; Van Maanen 1976).

Anticipatory socialization, which for faculty typically takes place during doctoral studies (Corcoran and Clark 1984; Freedman 1979), is the development of a positive orientation toward discipline-based and institutional norms, including broad social prescriptions and specific behavioral guidelines prevalent in the group to which the prospective faculty member aspires (Merton 1963). Thus, prior experiences and self-images must be modified to fit the demands of new roles and new group memberships. Acceptance by the group is facilitated by the newcomer's adopting the values, skills, and attitudes expected by peers (Merton 1963).

The nature of socialization processes varies across and within institutional types and discipline groups (Van Maanen 1976). Some typical steps in the socialization process have been identified, however: (1) identification of role models, (2) observation of role model behavior, (3) imitation of role model behavior, (4) evaluation by others of the "imitation," (5) modification of behavior in response to the evaluation, and (6) incorporation of values and behaviors of the role model into the newcomer's self-image (Bess 1978).

"People carry culture with them" (Van Maanen 1984, p. 217); that is, the patterns of understanding developed in other settings affect a newcomer's understanding of and response to tasks, perceived demands for performance, and social requirements of the new institution. Although the culture of the new or employing institution is maintained and perpetuated by teaching newcomers to view their workplace and social setting as they are viewed by culture bearers (Van Maanen and Schein

1979), the newcomers also shape, to some degree, the institutional culture.

Enactment

> *The story goes that three umpires disagreed about the task of calling balls and strikes. The first one said, "I calls them as they is." The second one said, "I calls them as I sees them." The third and cleverest umpire said, "They ain't nothin' till I calls them"* (Simons, cited in Weick 1979, p. 1).

The concept of enactment is consistent with the nonrational sociological view in that it emphasizes the active but unconscious role people play in creating their world. The process of enactment in organizations is explained as follows:

> *The manager literally "wades" into the swamp of events that surround him and actively tries to unrandomize them and impose order.... People in organizations try to sort this chaos into items, events, and parts, which are then connected, threaded into sequences, serially ordered, and related* (Weick 1979, p. 148).

Examples of enactment include self-fulfilling prophecy and socially constructed realities. In the latter, through conversations, actions, and negotiations, people create and give meaning to their environments. Because people are continually creating their own realities through various interpretive themes, an individual's experience is more than a personal assessment of an objective reality (Weick 1979). Thus, multiple realities are produced through individuals' sense-making processes, and people come to accept their enacted realities as "the way things are" (Morgan 1986). For example, organizational charts, job descriptions, and policy manuals can be perceived as "true" pictures of an organization, or they may be seen as symbolic representations of order developed to give the impression of institutional rationality to external audiences.

Summary
Culture is so complex that no single discipline can adequately illuminate its many facets. Anthropology, sociology, and allied

disciplines like social psychology and communications all contribute to a richer understanding of the culture of a college or university. Sociology and the sociocultural tradition in anthropology emphasize the role of formal organizational structures and collectives, such as work or clanlike groups, and less obvious behavior patterns (e.g., political economy) in transmitting the values and beliefs through which experience is made meaningful. The ideational tradition emphasizes the creation and transmission of culture through symbolic, mental imagery. Sociology has tended to emphasize how culture is influenced by formal structures and rational aspects of a college or university, such as job descriptions and formal hierarchies. Nonrational aspects of life in colleges and universities are acknowledged primarily in anthropology and, to a lesser degree, in sociology (e.g., enactment processes). These disciplines provide the foundation on which a framework can be developed to analyze the literature on culture in higher education.

Describing the culture of an organized setting as complex as a college or university is like peeling an onion. As one works through the many layers of an onion, from the outer skin to the core, the layers differ in texture and thickness, and it is not always obvious where one layer ends and the next begins. Similarly, using cultural lenses to examine and appreciate events and actions in a college or university and the behavior of members of various subgroups—faculty, administration, students, staff, women, and minorities—requires multiple layers of analysis.

Based on an understanding of the intellectual foundations of culture, the authors developed an analytical framework to guide a review of the literature on culture in higher education. Culture is complex, multifaceted, holistic, and paradoxical (e.g., substance and form, process and product, independent and dependent variable). Thus, the framework had to include as many elements of culture as possible, acknowledge the ecological characteristics of colleges and universities, and acknowledge historical events that shape and perpetuate institutional traditions and missions. And the framework had to accommodate multiple and sometimes conflicting theoretical positions, such as the phenomenological view from anthropology and the non-rational as well as the rational, structural views from sociology.

The framework had to reflect a balanced approach to cultural analysis, somewhere between acknowledging the holistic character of an institution's culture by describing cultural properties in phenomenological, almost ephemeral language and defining and describing very specifically every element of culture identified by cultural anthropologists, sociologists, and others that could conceivably be manifested in an institute of higher education. Cognizant that disaggregation and analysis independent of context (Bates 1987) are not always helpful (Kroeber and Kluckhohn 1952; Pettigrew 1979) and having been taught—nay, "socialized"—to seek the smallest identifiable human group to which comprehensive interpretative principles can be applied, the authors had to constantly remind themselves that "the study of cultures is always...a study of wholes, whether the[y] be of a society, a region, a university, or a department" (Taylor 1984, p. 126).

The framework described in this section provides for four layers of analysis and draws heavily on the work of Allaire and Firsirotu (1984), Becher (1984), Clark (1970), Clark et al. (1972), and Van Maanen and Barley (1985): (1) the external

Using cultural lenses to examine and appreciate events and actions in a college or university and the behavior of members of various subgroups requires multiple layers of analysis.

environment that surrounds a college or university; (2) the institution itself; (3) subcultures within the institution (e.g., faculty, professional staff) and within subcultures (e.g., faculty in the humanities and the sciences); and (4) individual actors and roles (e.g., university president). Such simplification admittedly runs the risk of underemphasizing the importance of holism and mutual shaping, properties that make culture a distinctive window on college and university life. But some solace can be found in the gentle admonition that the analysis of culture is "not an experimental science in search of laws but an interpretative one in search of meaning" (Geertz 1973, p. 5).

The External Environment

A college or university is ensconced within and influenced by a larger culture, a whole culture or society (Sanford 1962b) that is a composite of varying and overlapping subcultures—regional, economic, social, occupational, or some combination thereof. Viewed as open systems (Bertalanffy 1968; Peterson et al. 1986), colleges and universities are continually evolving, shaped by interactions between conditions in the external environment and the needs and concerns of groups within the institution (Tierney 1988). "When colleges change, it is usually because of outside influences. Thus, if we are interested in understanding the institution, we must identify and appreciate how the external environment shapes the institution" (Sanford 1962b, p. 73).

The first layer of analysis, the external environment, is grounded in ecological assumptions (Van Maanen and Barley 1985) and in theory and research about the outcomes of interactions between persons and environments (Astin and Holland 1961; Baird 1987; Barker and Gump 1964; Lewin 1936, 1951; Pace and Stern 1958; Pervin 1968; Stern 1970). The external environment includes numerous groups and agencies (e.g., governmental, occupational, professional, and accreditation associations) that have an interest in and influence on higher education (Education Commission 1980; Jencks and Riesman 1969; Kerr 1964; Riesman and Jencks 1962). The professionalization of occupations (Clark and Trow 1966), in the form of national, regional, and state associations, determines to a major extent areas of knowledge and skills that are addressed in the curriculum, particularly if accreditation is important to the viability of the field (e.g., law, medicine, education). Resources available to the institution and the importance of higher education to the nation's economic and political agendas also shape what transpires on a college campus (Kerr 1964).

Institutions of higher education in the United States are, generally speaking, products of western society in which masculine attributes like an orientation toward achievement and objectivity are valued over cooperation, connectedness, and subjectivity (Capra 1983; Ferguson 1980). The democratization of higher education is reflected in what students want from college (Brubacher and Rudy 1976; Clark and Trow 1966; Horowitz 1986; Levine 1986), such as a desire to make a lot of money and relatively little interest in developing a meaningful philosophy of life (Astin and Green 1987). One thesis is that the unprecedented growth of higher education in the United States between 1915 and 1940 was a reflection of the "culture of aspiration" (i.e., a college education was perceived as the path to economic well-being and social status) (Levine 1986). Prevailing attitudes and beliefs about the general purposes of higher education (e.g., to get a job, to live a better life, to tolerate differences among peoples, to appreciate the esthetic qualities of the natural world) affect how institutional leaders approach their work and how alumni feel about their alma mater.

As with other societal institutions, colleges are influenced by the media (Riesman and Jencks 1962). Recall, for example, the shift in societal attitudes about student activism that occurred between the early 1960s and the end of the Vietnam War (Brubacher and Rudy 1976). As more information was disseminated and the morality of the war was debated on television and in the print media, perceptions about the war changed, as did ultimately the policies of the U.S. government. Such pervasive shifts in societal attitudes surely influence events and the meanings given to them on the college campus. For example, some case studies of strategies for coping with decline suggest that an institution's response to student activism was one of a complicated set of factors associated with reduced alumni support (Chaffee 1983).

A common assertion is that the environment shapes behavior and attitudes (Lewin 1936; Sanford 1962a). Between 80 and 90 percent of those who attend college stay in their home state (Peterson and Smith 1979); thus, the mores of the host community or region of the country where a college is located influence the attitudes of students who attend the college. Whether an institution is in a major metropolitan area on the East Coast or on the outskirts of a small town in Iowa influences faculty and student behaviors that are tolerated and the degree of social cohesion developed.

The patterns of interaction of faculty and students are influenced by the surrounding community (Clark and Trow 1966). Some of the more experimental colleges (e.g., Bennington, Black Mountain, Goddard, Antioch, University of California–Santa Cruz) have been located in rural areas where students' identification with the institution is relatively easy to nurture, given the contrast with local residents and their way of life (i.e., the town-gown distinction). Of course, the success of Reed, Sarah Lawrence, and San Francisco State suggests that an innovative institution can also prosper in a suburban or metropolitan setting if buttressed by a courageous and committed faculty and administration (Clark and Trow 1966; Riesman and Jencks 1962).

Nevertheless, some institutions seem curiously out of place in their surroundings:

Seen from the hill at Amherst [College], Hampshire's curriculum is trendy, its standards lax, its faculty [comprised] largely of ideologues and misfits; its students take their education casually and are given credit for almost anything; it is a remnant of California counterculture, awkwardly grafted on the more civil New England scenery (Meister 1982, p. 27).

An institution's culture also reflects philanthropic interests and the institution's place among the economic elite (the haves and the have nots—Riesman and Jencks 1962). A base of "external believers" who provide resources—including moral support—to nurture the development of a distinctive institutional culture is important (Clark 1970). In addition, where an institution is placed in the empirically derived hierarchies of colleges and universities (Baldridge et al. 1977; Carnegie Foundation 1987), coupled with the degree to which an institution's image is salient to those other than the college's immediate constituent groups (e.g., alumni, faculty—Clark 1960), contribute to the development of a strong institutional culture.

In summary, an institutional culture is influenced by factors in the external environment, including economic conditions, societal attitudes and the role society expects higher education to play, the experiences and expectations of an institution's constituents (religious or ethnic sponsors, occupational or professional interest groups), and the institution's place in the economic and organizational hierarchy of American higher education. No one of these factors directly influences, in a linear sense, an institution's culture. Some have more or less influence, depending on the institution's age, size, financial stability, and so forth. Taken together, however, external factors influence in innumerable ways what receives attention and how meaning is made on a college campus.

The Institution

The second layer of analysis is the individual college or university, the primary focus of this report. An institution's culture evolves over time, shaped by patterns of routine interactions among students, faculty, institutional leaders (including founders), alumni, and other constituents. Culture is also influenced by the manner in which a college or university responds to external challenges that threaten the institution's viability (Riesman and Jencks 1962; Schein 1985). Thus, to understand and appreciate a college's culture, one must be familiar with its history—the college's original mission, its religious or ethnic heritage, and the circumstances under which the institution was founded (Clark 1970; Grant and Riesman 1978; Jencks and Riesman 1969; Riesman and Jencks 1962).

Saga

The institutional memory serves as the connective tissue between an institution's past and present and, to a considerable degree, shapes how future events will be interpreted. One illustration of institutional memory is Clark's description of organizational saga (1970, 1972), an institutionalized story that has evolved over time and describes critical events and individuals in the history of the institution (Masland 1985).

Saga, originally referring to a medieval Icelandic or Norse account of achievements and events in the history of a person or a group, has come to mean a narrative of heroic exploits, of a unique development that has deeply stirred the emotions of participants and descendants.... The term often refers also to the actual history itself, thereby including a stream of events, the participants, and the written or spoken interpretation. The element of belief is crucial, for without the credible story, the events and persons become history; with the development of belief, a particular bit of history be-

comes a definition full of pride and identity for the group (Clark 1972, p. 178).

Current events may influence the interpretation of aspects of the saga; however, if the saga is particularly salient, the saga may be invoked to legitimate, for example, governance and decision-making processes. The saga may take on legendary proportions (see table 1) if enough details or events are modified substantially through the retelling.

Academic program
The academic program is important to institutional culture:

When claims of distinctiveness are made, we hear most about the program... —special courses, unusual general education requirements, extraordinary modes of evaluation, unique ways of concentrating and spreading student effort.... The program core is subtly interconnected with other major components [such as] the beliefs of the faculty.... Academic men point to their decorated spears, their village totems, their bracelets signifying honor and beauty, and they speak proudly of the courses they have long embellished, the curricula they have lovingly fashioned by hand, and the trials they have devised for students to give great meaning to what otherwise would only be a paper credential. When they do so and do it so effectively that they convince themselves, the students, and many outsiders, the curriculum becomes rich with cultural meaning (Clark 1970, pp. 248–50).

A dedicated "personnel core" (Clark 1970)—a senior faculty—is critical to developing loyalty, commitment, and moral capital, all of which are integral components of a strong institutional culture. Faculty whose personal values as well as technical expertise are compatible with the central ideas and values of the institution is characteristic of the commitment. The socialization of newcomers by senior faculty is another strand in weaving the tapestry of institutional culture (Clark 1970).

Distinctive themes
A college's culture is a framework that helps faculty, students, alumni, and others to understand institutional events and activities, to create and define an internal self-image and external reputation, to develop loyalty and commitment, to acquire ex-

ternal resources for the college, and to generate "moral capital," a deep belief in the value of the institution that gives direction to institutional leaders and supporters in times of crises (Clark 1984). In this sense, a strong culture may engender a feeling of community reflected by "a capacity for relatedness within individuals—relatedness not only to people but to events in history, to nature, to the world of ideas, and...to things of the spirit" (Palmer 1987, p. 24).

Deeply held beliefs and guiding principles may develop into an institutional ethos, an underlying attitude that describes how faculty and students feel about themselves; this attitude is comprised of the moral and aesthetic aspects of culture that reflect and set the tone, character, and quality of institutional life. A distinctive institutional ethos has five themes: (1) accurately and reflectively self-aware, (2) empathically responsive, (3) internally coherent, (4) stably resilient, and (5) autonomously distinctive (Heath 1981). These themes are congruent with the characteristics of colleges that have high faculty morale (Rice and Austin 1988).

Ethos is different from the world view shared by faculty and other institutional agents. The world view or *Weltanschauung* (like the concept of paradigm discussed earlier) is a "picture of the way things in sheer actuality are, their concept of nature, of self, of society. It contains their most comprehensive ideas of order" (Geertz 1973, p. 127), the way in which the basic postulates of a culture are organized so as to be comprehensible (Hoebel 1966).

> [An institution's ethos] is made intellectually reasonable by being shown to represent a way of life implied by the actual state of affairs [that] the world view describes, and the world view is made emotionally acceptable by being presented as an image of an actual state of affairs of which such a way of life is an authentic expression (Geertz 1973, p. 127).

Organizational characteristics

Not all colleges have a distinctive institutional ethos (Clark 1960), and the differences between colleges and universities in the United States are not as striking as their similarities (Carnegie Council 1980). Accordingly, institutional distinctiveness is more propaganda than fact (Chase 1980). *Demise of Diversity* provides some empirical support for this position by concluding that the attitudes of alumni from different kinds of colleges and universities became less distinct between 1950 and 1970 (Pace 1974). Nevertheless, the weight of the evidence suggests that institutional distinctiveness is a viable manifestation of the concept of culture (cf. Bowen 1977; Clark 1970; Heath 1968; Jencks and Riesman 1962; Riesman and Jencks 1962).

Institutional size (Clark 1970; Heath 1968; Kuh 1981) and complexity, perceived or "real," seem to be inversely related to the development of an ethos (Allaire and Firsirotu 1984; Clark 1970; Clark and Trow 1966). Larger institutions of higher education tend to be more complex structurally, which impedes development of a coherent picture or tone (Peterson et al. 1986). When the number of faculty, administrators, and support staff approaches one or two thousand and the physical plant includes a significant number (40 or 50) of widely dispersed buildings, informal contact among students, faculty, and other institutional agents is diminished (Clark et al. 1972).

Formal structure is less important in a small college because it determines only a minor part of the significant interactions between institutional agents, students, and other members of the college's community (Clark et al. 1972). Curricular structures and academic requirements may be less important than other institutional features like mission, size, complexity, and students' motivation, aspirations, and ability. For example, a small liberal arts college with 1,000 students and a relatively strong affiliation with the founding church body could be host to a homogenous institutional culture, a situation where all members of an organization subscribe to the same normative order and where the normative order can be distinguished only in contrast to another college (Van Maanen and Barley 1984). Whether an institution reflects a monolithic culture depends on the degree to which faculty and students interpret or make meaning of events and actions in a similar way. (Some examples of such institutional cultures are provided in the next section.)

Other factors
Most universities have more than one dominant subculture that inhibits emergence of a distinctive institutional ethos, which is not to say that elements of culture do not exist at large institutions (see Wells 1980; Zwerling 1988). Institutional artifacts are obvious (e.g., the athletic fight song, school colors, and recorded histories of the alma mater) and have numerous meanings for constituents.

Temporal factors may influence an institution's culture. Technological changes in teaching and learning processes, turbulence in the external environment (Tierney 1988), and cataclysmic events such as damage to the physical plant resulting from natural disaster (Peterson et al. 1986; Rice and Austin 1988) present opportunities and cultural challenges (Sanford 1962b). At certain points in the history of an institution, leaders may consider some aspects of the culture to be antithetical to their vision of the changes the institution must make to remain viable (Clark 1970). In the 1960s, many church-related colleges, to accommodate the social interests of increasing numbers of students from the first wave of baby boomers, allowed dancing on campus for the first time, thus significantly changing the culture. (The next section describes how presidents Aydelotte at Swarthmore (Clark 1970; Clark and Trow 1966) and Hopkins at Wabash (Trippet 1982) successfully challenged the dominant student culture in the 1920s by deemphasizing athletics and increasing the academic rigor of the curriculum.)

An institution's ethos, academic traditions, and heroes are powerful cultural determinants. How faculty and students spend their time, with whom they interact, what people "perceive" the culture to be, and the manner in which the norms and values of the institution shape behavior in the midst of crises seem to be key aspects of institutional culture.

Subcultures

Culture exists in "any size of social unit that has had the opportunity to learn and stabilize its view of itself and the environment around it" (Schein 1985, p. 8). If a group of people have shared a significant number of important experiences in responding to problems imposed by the external environment or by internal conflicts, such common experiences will probably encourage the group to develop a similar view of the institution and their place in it. Further, the value system of the group may differ from that of the host culture, providing further bonding for the group.

[The shared view of the group] has to have worked for long enough to have come to be taken for granted and to have dropped out of awareness. Culture in this sense is a learned product of group experience and is, therefore, to be found only where there is to be a definable group with a significant history (Schein 1985, p. 7).

At least three types of subcultures exist within a dominant culture: enhancing, orthogonal, and countercultural (Martin and Siehl 1983). An enhancing subculture adheres to the institution's core values more fervently than the rest of the members of the college. Senior faculty are more likely to use the organizational saga to interpret current circumstances (Clark 1972). On one campus, the professors of distinguished rank meet regularly and serve as informal advisers to the president; such a group would be an enhancing subculture if their advice and actions served to perpetuate core institutional values and discouraged initiatives that would change the mission of the institution.

Faculty using particle accelerators to conduct research in high-energy physics may be an orthogonal subculture if they "simultaneously accept the core values of the [institution] and a separate, unconflicting set of values particular to themselves" (Martin and Siehl 1983, p. 53). Student affairs staff on many campuses may also make up an orthogonal culture. They implement institutional policies and, at the same time, are committed to encouraging the intellectual and social-emotional development of students through out-of-class experiences (National Association 1987).

A subculture becomes countercultural when it poses a direct threat to the values of the institution. Countercultures thrive in an open, risk-free environment like that typically provided by a college or university. For example, radical groups, such as the Students for Democratic Society, were common on many campuses in the 1960s (Brubacher and Rudy 1976; Horowitz 1987). Even conforming or orthogonal enclaves, such as the faculty senate, may challenge aspects of the dominant culture. Some high-profile, formally recognized student organizations (e.g., fraternities, athletic teams) manifest values antithetical to institutional aims. Whether the existence of countercultures becomes debilitating depends on many factors (Van Maanen and Barley 1984), some of which are discussed later.

Within a college or university, numerous subcultures may be operating (Tierney 1988): managerial, discipline-based faculty groups (e.g., humanities or natural sciences), professional staff (e.g., student affairs workers), social groups of faculty and students, and peer groups created by physical proximity of living quarters or special interests (e.g., music, athletics). Faculty offices are usually arranged by discipline, a factor that reinforces what is considered important to study, how knowledge is created and disseminated, and how meaning is made of information (Becher 1984; Mitroff and Kilmann 1978). Physical proximity may also contribute to the evolution of shared understandings and work norms (Newcomb 1962; Van Maanen and Barley 1984).

Professional groups have different paradigms or ways of viewing the world and differ in what they perceive to be the primary business of the institution. At a major research university, physics faculty may see their primary role as research and attach little value to professional service. On the other hand, business and education faculty at the same institution may place a higher value on service—which is not to say that all professional school faculty view their responsibilities in the same way. The business faculty may define "service" as consulting with major corporations (and earn one or more times their academic-year salary from consulting), while education faculty may view their work with public schools as a professional obligation or courtesy.

Subcultures sometimes form within subcultures. Schisms in disciplines sometimes begin when members cluster themselves on the basis of different views toward the discipline. For example, legal realists, sometimes called "Crits," have argued against the classical view of law as rational and neutral; rather, they assert, the law is indeterminate, political, and susceptible to the biases of judges, juries, and lawyers. The position adopted by Crits has alienated them from their colleagues who hold to the classical view of law (Coughlin 1985). In a college or university, the antagonism between subgroups may sometimes become so intense that members of the two camps stop talking and become, for all practical purposes, two subcultures "delimited mainly by their scorn for one another" (Van Maanen and Barley 1984, p. 344).

Individual Actors
Faculty, students, and administrators are not merely passive recipients of the predetermined logic and sense-making mechanisms of an institution's culture. All institutional agents participate in constructing a coherent picture of what is going on in the institution. The extent to which faculty and students identify with the institution and are culturally competent (i.e., they share meanings and beliefs with others—Allaire and Firsirotu 1984, p. 225) is continually changing. Because the same cultural material is available to faculty and staff (i.e., they are more or less aware of the history and traditions, current poli-

cies and practices, and so forth), however, considerable overlap can be expected in their beliefs and assumptions.

Any individual can contribute to and shape the meaning given to an event in a college or university. The influence of dominant actors, such as presidents or founding fathers, on culture is documented in countless institutional histories (cf. Baker 1978; Clark 1970; Green 1979; Nelson 1961; Peckham 1967). The stories and myths told about these institutional leaders shape, over time, the interpretation of issues, policies, and governance structures. Institutional agents other than a president or CEO can also be influential in shaping institutional culture. Richard Moll, a successful admissions director at Bowdoin and Vassar, was brought to the University of California at Santa Cruz to change the institution's "flaky, touchy-feely" image. Moll turned the university's vice—its image as a campus that attracted wacky, liberal students—into a virtue by marketing the institution as an innovative, distinctive, single-purpose campus in zealous pursuit of traditional academic rigor and excellence (Adams 1984). (The next section provides a few more examples of individuals who are credited with shaping an institution's culture.)

Summary
The framework developed to review the higher education literature acknowledges that the culture of an institution of higher education evolves from an interplay between the external environment and an institution's history, its formal organization, the attitudes faculty and students bring with them, and the beliefs they acquire about the college. Thus, a college reflects, to varying degrees, the values and accepted practices of the host society and those of constituents external to the institution (e.g., parents and governmental officials) and internal (faculty, administrators, and students). The conditions under which an institution was established and the convictions of founders and subsequent leaders may nurture the development of a distinctive ethos that is then reinforced by faculty and student beliefs and behaviors consistent with the sense of purpose and values on which the ethos is based. Few colleges are monolithic entities; dominant subcultures and subgroupings within them shape the institutional culture. The next section provides specific illustrations from the literature about how various elements of culture are manifested in colleges and universities.

THREADS OF INSTITUTIONAL CULTURE

The examples of institutional culture provided in this section are representative; not every property of culture identified in preceding sections is illustrated, although examples of most surely could be found. And although documentary films and major motion pictures depict aspects of culture in colleges and universities, the examples used in this chapter are from the published literature on higher education, such as ubiquitous institutional histories (cf. Gard 1970; Nelson 1961; Nollen 1953; Peckham 1967) and institutional ethnographies (cf. Grant and Riesman 1978; Keeton and Hilberry 1969; Riesman and Jencks 1962). Memoirs of college and university presidents (cf. Trippet 1982; Wells 1980) and faculty (cf. Baker 1978) also can be rich sources of material about institutional culture. In addition, some historical accounts of the development of higher education in the United States (cf. Brubacher and Rudy 1976; Horowitz 1984; Veysey 1965) include references—albeit usually indirect—to institutional culture.

Few published works describe colleges and universities with the level of detail needed to reveal cultural elements.

Because only a handful of scholars have studied colleges and universities from the point of view of an anthropologist (Riesman and Jencks 1962), few published works describe colleges and universities with the level of detail needed to reveal cultural elements. The best of them include Clark's description of three liberal arts colleges (1970), Riesman and Jencks's ethnographies of four institutions (1962) (although the level of detail is thin), books by London (1978) and Weis (1985) on the culture of community colleges, Tierney's work on the semiotics of leadership (1987), and the institutional vignettes that occasionally appear in *Change* magazine (e.g., Adams 1984; Meister 1982; Rice and Austin 1988; Riesman 1981a; Zwerling 1988).

The examples are organized according to seven features of institutional culture that have been emphasized in the literature: (1) historical roots, including religious convictions of founders, and external influences, particularly the support of the institution's constituents (e.g., alumni, philanthropic sponsors); (2) the academic program, including curricular emphases; (3) the personnel core, including faculty and other institutional agents who contribute to the maintenance of the institution's culture; (4) the social environment, particularly the influence of dominant student subculture(s); (5) artifactual manifestations of culture, such as architecture, customs, ceremonies, and rituals; (6) distinctive themes that reflect the institution's core values and beliefs transmitted by the ethos, norms, and saga; and (7) individual actors, such as founders or charismatic leaders.

In keeping with the holistic, shaping properties of culture, the features should not be viewed as mutually exclusive; each influences the others. An institution's historical roots, for example, influence the curriculum, artifacts, and institutional ethos in pervasive ways. The primary purpose of this section is to illustrate aspects of culture rather than to demonstrate how the elements work together to form a "whole" institutional culture.

Historical Roots and External Influences
History and institutional culture are inextricably intertwined.

Religious beliefs
Threads of continuity and shared action, particularly at private or independent institutions, often have had origins in religious purposes and are reflected by faculty values, by curriculum requirements, and by the characteristics of students who are attracted to the institution (Clark and Trow 1966; Riesman and Jencks 1962). Most major religious groups established one or more colleges. For example, Jews founded Brandeis; Catholics established about 300 colleges (Riesman and Jencks 1962), including Georgetown, St. Louis University, Notre Dame, and St. Ambrose; Lutherans founded Augustana College in Illinois and in South Dakota, Gettysburg, Capital, Pacific Lutheran, Wartburg, and Wittenberg; Mennonites created Goshen; Congregationalists established Amherst, Dartmouth, and Oberlin; Methodists established Albion, Asbury (now DePauw), Duke, University of the Pacific, Wesleyan in Connecticut and in Georgia; and Presbyterians founded Davidson, Lafayette, and Princeton (Tewksbury 1965). Many of these colleges were established to perpetuate distinctive beliefs of the founding group (Jencks and Riesman 1969), and to maintain a unitary belief system, faculty were sought who had the same faith as the founders.

Ethnic considerations also spawned "the multiplication of church colleges, with French Canadians, for example, preferring Assumption College in Worcester to 'Irish' Holy Cross or Boston College, or with Swedes supporting Gustavus Adolphus in Minnesota against neighboring Norwegian St. Olaf" (Riesman and Jencks 1962, p. 96). Supporters in the early days of St. Olaf used the college to create a "little Norway" and to prepare teachers and ministers. The sons and daughters of Norse immigrant families were sent to St. Olaf to become "citizens who could move with some sophistication in the market-place and the town meeting" (Clark et al. 1972, p. 38).

The founders' reasons for establishing a religious college may no longer be obvious. In many church-related institutions, the proportion of students and faculty who are members of the founding faith has decreased (Jencks and Riesman 1969). Nevertheless, ceremonies and events continue to reflect traditions of the founding groups. For example, 1,500 of the 2,000 students at Luther College participate in the annual performance of Handel's *Messiah*; lutefisk, lefsa, and apple pie topped with cheese are served as part of holiday festivities. These and other artifacts of Norwegian heritage combine to create an ambience at the small college in northeast Iowa that is different from that of California Lutheran College in Thousand Oaks, California, or Wagner College in Staten Island, New York, although all three are affiliated with the Lutheran church.

Evangelical colleges, such as Berry, Berea, and Mars Hill, "serve as decompression chambers that make the passage from home to the larger world less traumatic for the shy or the provincial" (Riesman 1981a, p. 19) and ameliorate culture shock on the part of adolescents who leave the protective womb of the family and home church. It is no accident that Brigham Young University is located in areas heavily populated by Mormons and that Wake Forest and Berry were established in an area with many Southern Baptists. Mormons send their sons and daughters to Brigham Young so that their children can acquire credentials for the working world and find a mate without compromising their faith (Connell 1983). Similarly, "conservative Free Methodists do not want the Southern Baptists to capture their young; they maintain both their churches and colleges in a struggle among denominations, each of which is evangelical in a different way..." (Riesman 1981a, p. 18).

The mores of the supporting religious body are manifested in codes of student conduct (often enforced by students themselves), mandatory courses in religion, and a sedate social life usually marked by the absence of alcohol and drugs. As Catholics once sent their offspring exclusively to Fordham, St. John's in New York, or Holy Cross, fundamentalist parents send their children to Bob Jones University because smoking, drinking alcohol, listening to rock music, dancing, card playing, going to public movie theaters (regardless of what is showing), kissing or holding hands with a date, and interracial dating and marriage are banned (Connell 1983). Male and female students are prohibited from walking together unless they have a legitimate reason to be going in the same direction. One senior said that such rules "sound absolutely crazy" when taken out of context. "When my [older] sister came I thought she was crazy.... But when I came down to campus I found it was completely different.... It's worth the extra work to be able to get the Christian philosophy for at least four years just to make me stronger in what I believe is right and how I want to live" (Connell 1983, p. 42).

Evangelical colleges provide an option to students who would feel like misfits on a secular, cosmopolitan campus. Parents are willing to pay the disproportionate cost of a private education to protect their children from worldly contamination (Connell 1983). Thus, "evangelical colleges offer a partial and temporary escape from freedom—an enclave that is neither total nor totalitarian" (Riesman 1981a, p. 20).

Social attitudes

During the 1960s, attempts were made to create collegiate cultures that reflected the open, responsive, learning environment characteristic of the free education movement popular during that period (cf. MacDonald 1973). These colleges emphasized experiential learning and encouraged students to collaborate with faculty in determining course content (Meister 1982). One such experimental institution was Kresge College, the sixth liberal arts college at the University of California–Santa Cruz (Grant and Riesman 1978). Most of Kresge's founders were directly influenced by the encounter and T-group movements; many had participated in National Training Laboratory or esalen encounter workshops and were influenced by the Rogerian theory about community and freedom. Indeed, "if Kresge College could have adopted the name of its patron saint rather than its benefactor, it would have been called Carl Rogers College" (Grant and Riesman 1978, p. 77).

A distinguished microbiologist at Cal Tech, the first provost of Kresge College, outlined his intentions. The college was to be:

...a participatory, consensual democracy.... All members of the community have the right to participate in the decisions that will affect them; ...no decision will be reached to which even one individual was opposed, whether he be provost or freshman.... Collective human activities are tremendously af-

fected by the quality of interactions between people. I believe that placing a high priority on enhancing the quality of interpersonal interactions in the college will result in an exciting, productive, and creative learning community (Grant and Riesman 1978, p. 80).

The Kresge College counterpart to the commune, which was associated in the popular press in the 1960s with drug use and free love, was the kin group, sometimes called the family. Each kin group, comprised of 15 to 20 members, including the faculty advisor, lived, worked, cooked, and kept house together. The kin group was also the basic political unit of the college and was represented on decision-making bodies. In addition, the kin group was a seminar unit of the Kresge core curriculum (Grant and Riesman 1978).

About the same time, but on the other coast, another innovative institution, Hampshire College, was born in response to students' discontent.

Hampshire's aim was to replace the classroom by independent work as the central learning experience.... Progress was made by examination, meaning that each student was to submit a piece of independent work to a faculty committee [that], after a process of tutorial instruction, would evaluate the student's work and decide, in consultation with the student, whether he or she was now ready to move to the next of three levels of study. The last level...required the student to do a major project, comparable to the effort of a senior honors thesis..., proof of integrative or interdisciplinary study, and community service. There were initially no time limits on this progress through college, although the assumption was that four years was about right.

With the rapid decline of student dissent in the seventies, the rise of inflation, the overall decline in enrollments, and the shift in middle-class attitudes from affluence to scarcity consciousness, the applicant pool began to dry up. There were fewer of the educationally prepared and ideologically committed students available as alternative high school programs disappeared (Meister 1982, pp. 29–30).

Both Kresge and Hampshire reflected the liberal social attitudes of the times.

Academic Program

The curriculum and the academic climate of an institution are influenced in large measure by what faculty, students, and external audiences perceive to be important in the process of teaching and learning. One author describes how the curriculum shaped the academic experience at Yale (Catlin 1982), and the ethnographies of several liberal arts colleges developed by Grant and Riesman (1978) reflect elements of institutional culture influenced by the curriculum.

For example, a half century ago, St. John's "adopted a radically revolutionary program of required study of great books, language, science, and mathematics" (*Bulletin of St. John's College*, cited in Grant and Riesman 1978, p. 40). That curriculum has remained virtually unchanged, even though more than half of the St. John's students leave before graduation (the attrition rate at most selective liberal arts colleges is under 25 percent (Hossler 1984). The curriculum and the out-of-class lives of students are well integrated, particularly Sunday evening through Friday evening. Students are in class between 15 and 20 hours a week. On Monday and Thursday evenings, all students and faculty participate in a "Great Books" seminar. Friday evening includes a formal lecture attended by most of the faculty, many faculty spouses, and students. On the weekend, St. Johnnies behave just like young people elsewhere— loud music, drinking, dancing, and other forms of relaxation. But by Sunday afternoon, the demands of the curriculum take over and students turn their attention and energies to the academic program once again (Grant and Riesman 1978).

At some colleges, the religious interests of the founding denomination continue to influence the curriculum. For example, during the 1960s, religion and philosophy courses were required of all Catholic students at Portland University and of all students at St. Olaf and Luther colleges. The emphasis on religion in the curriculum also is reflected in the values of students attracted to the institution and its graduates. In colleges with required courses in religion, most students maintain the religious convictions they exhibited at the time of matriculation. At institutions with a limited emphasis on religion, students tend to become more liberal in their religious orientation (Clark et al. 1972).

Occupational interest groups also influence the curriculum and shape institutional culture (Riesman and Jencks 1962; Veysey 1965). At Harvard in the early 1800s, the curriculum emphasized Greek and Latin, languages used by clergy. In the late 1800s, when mandatory schooling became popular, more children stayed in school longer and created a demand for teachers, which in turn led to a proliferation of normal schools. The demand for teachers was so great that many liberal arts colleges introduced courses in pedagogy.

The land-grant movement (see Edmond 1978) created a new generation of colleges committed to increasing access to members of underrepresented groups and to responding to the needs of a more diverse industrial and economic system. J.R. Williams, the first president of the first land-grant college, Michigan State University, authorized the construction of three buildings: "College Hall with offices, classrooms, library, and laboratory; Saint's Rest with rooms and dining halls for housing students; and a brick barn for housing the farm animals" (Edmond 1978, p. 8). But the presence of animals on the campus did little to deemphasize the liberal arts tradition; the development of the "whole man" continued to occupy a prominent place in the curriculum at Michigan State and other land-grant colleges (Jencks and Riesman 1969; Veysey 1965).

As a distinctive feature of an institution, the curriculum can have a pervasive influence on the dominant student culture. In the 1920s, students at most colleges were from nearby towns (Brubacher and Rudy 1976). This feature was true of Swarthmore College, which was founded by a liberal wing of the Quakers. As with other institutions at that time, the collegiate version of the "good life" flourished (Brubacher and Rudy 1976); the academic program was, at best, a second priority to participation in a glee club or a secret fraternity and cheering on the football team, which had a schedule "so imposing as to drag the college into the sports scandals that were becoming a regular adjunct of American higher education" (Clark et al. 1972, p. 34).

In an effort to change the image of the institution, President Frank Aydelotte, with the help of the faculty, implemented a modified Oxford scheme in which selected juniors and seniors could participate in special intensive seminars, the "honors" concept. The college began to offer scholarships to serious, intellectually able students with a capacity for leadership. The faculty and new students gradually but drastically modified social activities. Freshman hazing was eliminated and the number of fraternity dances drastically reduced; in 1933, sororities were abolished. The administration and faculty gradually assumed control over athletics and transformed a program of big-time intercollegiate sports into one of intramural intercollegiate sports for the student amateur. The financial support of the sports program was changed from gate receipts to a college subsidy (Clark 1970; Clark et al. 1972). Swarthmore became an academically respectable place to attend college, because through Aydelotte's leadership, the college fully embraced the life of serious study.

Reed College established a conference system of instruction. A teacher and a few students discussed the readings around a seminar table. Students were responsible for leading the discussion, interpreting the readings, and explaining and defending their interpretations of the material (Mitzman 1979). Major academic hurdles were institutionalized (e.g., an examination for entry into the senior year, a senior year thesis, and an oral examination before graduation) to emphasize the importance of consistent and serious study. Reed's emphasis on intellectuality continues to emphasize the study of science; it was, in 1979, the only undergraduate college in the nation with its own nuclear reactor used by faculty and students in their research (Mitzman 1979).

The Personnel Core

In most colleges and universities, the faculty assume responsibility for program quality, asserting they are the only group authorized to establish and modify academic programs and policy. In this sense, faculty, particularly the group(s) viewed by their colleagues as opinion leaders, are influential in maintaining and enriching the institution's culture. At colleges and universities with elaborate academic governing structures, faculty often use processes of governance—sometimes intentionally, sometimes unwittingly—to minimize disruptive change in the institution's culture that may include innovations proposed by the administrtion. In this sense, faculty can be a conservative force; they are just as likely to lobby on behalf of traditions of mediocrity as to vigorously pursue new policies that encourage scholarship and high intellectual standards (Clark and Trow 1966).

City College of New York (CUNY) was founded in 1847 as the first free municipal institution of higher education in the United States with a humanistic mission; it subsequently became a monument to a "culture of aspiration" (Levine 1986).

City College served as a unique bridge between the people

*who came from the old world and the America that was in
the process of being built.... [It was] the gathering place for
people from lower echelons of the economic and social system; that is what makes it a unique college, a democratic
college* (Harburg, cited in Marshak 1981, p. 13).

City College provided graduates with intellectual training,
professional skills, and academic credentials needed for social
mobility and postgraduate achievement.

But as New York City changed, so did CUNY. Large numbers of blacks and Hispanics settled in surrounding neighbor-
hoods. At the very time that many people of color became
interested in attending college, the quality of public schools began to deteriorate rapidly. In the late 1960s, student unrest became prevalent throughout CUNY. At that time, one of the
most complicated and controversial policy matters in CUNY's
history—open admissions—was implemented. As a consequence, the college's educational mission was radically altered.

To respond to the enrollment of increasing numbers of students from educationally disadvantaged backgrounds, CUNY
attempted to provide extensive remediation, tutorial assistance,
individualized counseling, and additional financial aid (Marshak
1981). The chair of the English Department hired 21 additional
full-time faculty members in one three-month period to teach
basic writing—in a department that once offered 70 percent of
its courses in literature. After the open admissions policy was
implemented, two-thirds of the English courses covered basic
written composition (Gross 1978). The influx of ill-prepared
students required faculty to teach in ways for which they had
not been trained (Marshak 1981).

*The faculty experienced a shock of cultural recognition....
The older professors who struggled to teach sentence fragments were scarcely appeased; they would not change. The
younger faculty...were academic schizophrenics holding what
seemed to be two opposing ideas—literacy and literature—in
their mind at the same time* (Gross 1978, p. 17).

Many faculty, unable or unwilling to change their instructional
approach to accommodate remedial efforts, went about business
as usual with unproductive results (Marshak 1981).

Another illustration of the role faculty play in maintaining
the institutional culture is the clash between faculty and admin-

istration at the Rhode Island School of Design (RISD) (Cummings 1978). RISD's faculty was comprised essentially of artists and craftspeople. In 1975, a new president was appointed with a mandate from the trustees to exercise more authority over operations to deal with conditions related to the decreasing pool of traditional-age college students. Shortly after her arrival, the new president reorganized the administration:

> *setting up vice presidencies with formal lines of communication in a "top down" corporate fashion. On the academic side, she conferred regularly only with her provost and six division chiefs. During her first two years, she attended only two of the faculty's monthly meetings,...[a] style of governing [that] antagonized many* (Cummings 1978, p. 34).

The new management style sharply conflicted with the informal, collegial approach to matters faculty had come to expect. Although a formal censure of the president failed, faculty dissatisfaction increased. At commencement, the faculty—including a crimson-robed division chair—cheered the senior class speaker, who assailed the president's autocratic behavior (Cummings 1978).

Because faculty are the carriers of institutional culture, selective recruitment and retention of faculty whose values are congruent with the culture of the institution are critical. When institutional leaders wish to modify the institution's mission, cooperation and support of the faculty is indispensable. In these instances, cultural elements must also be altered. While a single leader, such as a college president, can initiate innovative changes, the ideas will be slow to take hold unless powerful members of the faculty "remain committed while the initiator is present and especially after [the leader] is gone" (Clark 1970, p. 246).

Social Environment
The social environment of a college is an important element of culture because it contributes to the institution's external image. An institution with a salient image (Clark 1960) has the capacity to attract a particular kind of student, thereby shaping the student mix, the climate of the campus, and the effects of the college on students and faculty, and attracting external resources (Hossler 1984; Kuh 1977; Peterson et al. 1986; Riesman and Jencks 1962). Through decades of performance, a

college's public reputation or image is established (Clark et al. 1972):

Students are important to the character of the institution in that they are the material for much of its work.... They come with personal inclinations and then informally relate to one another in patterns that uphold the predispositions or alter them. As a result...the student body becomes a major force in defining the institution (Clark 1970, p. 253).

As early as the 1950s, the typical Reed College student was known as a bearded, barefoot, nonconforming intellectual critical of prevailing social norms (Clark et al. 1972). Reed's first president, William T. Foster, established enduring ideals and policies that discouraged intercollegiate sports and any form of social life that would compete with the classroom; sororities and fraternities were banned. Reed's image of liberal intellectualism subsequently attracted liberal but academically serious students and faculty; the college also gained a reputation for its strong academic programs. Reed's students may be unequaled in their belief in the distinctiveness of their campus and actively resist institutional policies that threaten the college's culture. In the early 1950s, for example, then-president Ballantine attempted to redefine students' role in administering the honor system. Ballantine suggested the administration should share the responsibility for student affairs through his office as well as the dean of students. Student leaders preferred that the Student Council maintain control over student behavior, and representatives of the senior class wrote to alumni protesting administrative interference (Clark 1970).

When two or more dominant student subcultures exist, students' out-of-class experiences may be enriched. When this condition is met, students have different subgroups with which to identify and be challenged by attitudes and behaviors characteristic of the other dominant subculture(s). The existence of multiple subcultures also allows opportunities for several "heroes" to emerge, peers that students wish to emulate. The existence of more than one hero provides students with several ways to succeed in the eyes of their peers (Clark et al. 1972). At Swarthmore, the hero was a "very bright student, seriously academic and intellectual, who won such academic prizes as finishing high in the honors competition. The athlete, the campus politician, the Don Juan, the future corporation president

The existence of multiple subcultures also allows opportunities for several "heroes" to emerge, peers that students wish to emulate.

were not serious competitors for the status of hero. Yet, along with this cultural consensus, some diversity remain[ed], some room for subheroes" (Clark et al. 1972, p. 320). President Aydelotte's successful reform efforts required the transformation of the dominant student subculture. Indeed, the whole experiment would have failed if the students' style of life had not been radically altered through a number of mutually reinforcing interventions.

Similarly, Wabash College in the early 1900s was characterized by a "caveman" caricature that came from its dominance over Big Ten and other major university athletic teams. Almost all student financial aid was administered by the athletic department and went to athletes in the form of scholarships and college jobs. That policy was drastically changed under President Hopkins, who was determined to modernize the curriculum, increase academic rigor, attract higher-quality students and faculty, clean up the caveman ambience of the place, and establish a reputation of integrity for the college. Hopkins outlawed the "Rhynie Up," in which "all freshmen passed meekly through the gauntlet of the senior class and had their bottoms beaten black and blue with hickory paddles" (Trippet 1982, p. 17). Because of more rigorous admission requirements, including foreign language, Wabash began to attract a very different type of student. In 1929, like Aydelotte of Swarthmore and other college presidents at the time (Brubacher and Rudy 1976), Hopkins took a position unpopular with alumni and townspeople: He brought the finances and administration of athletics under the direct control of the college administration (Trippet 1982). Through these and allied changes, extracurricular activities at Wabash became subordinated to, and integrated with, a life of more serious study, one that deemphasized sports and social life. Intellectualism became a virtue; the energy formerly directed toward competitive sports was transferred toward academic achievement.

Swarthmore and Wabash are extreme but persuasive cases of the ways in which academic purposes can permeate and influence the social climate. The values of dominant student subcultures today at Swarthmore and Wabash continue to reflect the positions adopted a half century ago by institutional leaders and faculty (Clark and Trow 1966; Clark et al. 1972; Trippet 1982). The recent anti-intellectual behavior of social fraternities on some campuses indicates that student culture remains an important area of concern for administrators and faculty.

Artifacts

The culture of a college or university is reflected by artifacts, observable manifestations of values and beliefs. This section presents examples from two categories of artifacts: (1) architecture and (2) ceremonials, rites, and rituals.

Architecture

The physical environment reflects distinctive values and aspirations of those who live and work in a college (Sturner 1972). "If we are going to set high educational standards, then our architecture should reflect those standards. If we teach culture, we must be purveyors of culture as well" (Polshek, cited in Williams 1985, p. 55). In the United States, a college campus is expected to be "a distinctive place whose architecture is at once historic and monumental—a source of pride and affiliation" (Thelin and Yankovich 1987, p. 57).

> *Whether a revered landmark, a quiet oak-lined quadrangle, or the historic disarray of fraternity row, the images evoke lives lived and years past. We want them to remain, and, indeed, college campuses have been good repositories of memory.... Whatever the age or setting or spread, college campuses tell the history and settlement of the region, a sequence of distinctive places with buildings that can be read like books. An autumn stroll through a campus—especially with a good guide—can be suffused with history as light through coloring leaves, as stirring to the spirit as it is to the senses* (Morris 1983, p. 82).

The expectation that a college campus be a distinctive architectural form can be extended to community colleges as well. Miami-Dade College, an institution of 100,000 students and four major campuses, is the largest community college in the world (Zwerling 1988). Consonant with the balmy southern Florida climate, each campus has atria, breezeways, lagoons, fountains, and sidewalk cafes. Although the buildings on the four campuses are similar, Miami-Dade students are quick to point out that the South campus "looks like a real college campus" with vast parking lots, green spaces between buildings, and other "accoutrements of affluence" (Zwerling 1988, p. 19).

Alma Mater discusses the influence of architecture on the behavior of faculty and students in 10 women's colleges between

1830 and 1930 (Horowitz 1984). The physical plant of each college was designed to fulfill a special academic and social mission (Thelin and Yankovich 1987). The dining hall, for example, offered an opportunity for classes to demonstrate cohesiveness through group cheers yet could be transformed for banquets and promenades. In addition to the reshaping of the indoor physical spaces for particular events, outdoor spaces also had symbolic purposes. "Each college had its particular paths, its favorite haunts and retreats. The lake, the circle, or even the stretches of countryside beyond campus bounds became special places for important conversations or self-examinations" (Horowitz 1984, p. 170).

> *A stranger to the handsome [Bryn Mawr] campus might be struck by "the grand old stone buildings covered with ivy, by the campus stretching far off into the distance, and by the great spreading trees." As impressive as the scene appears, "how much more then must it mean to those who have lived in those halls, studied in the library under those trees, and discussed the problems of life, death, and eternity in cloisters...; each room, each tree, almost each corner is bound up with some special memory.... Through ritual, students symbolically claimed college ground. Whatever the intentions of founders and builders, in the minds of students—and thus of future alumnae—the buildings and landscape of the women's college became material embodiment of college life* (Horowitz 1984, pp. 175, 178).

In the lore of many institutions are stories about natural disasters, such as fires or tornadoes, that have damaged or destroyed college structures (cf. Clark 1970; Horowitz 1984; Trippet 1982). Discussions about whether to replace or repair the building were often spirited. Yet either decision—to renovate or to build a new structure—could be rationalized and was used to instill loyalty and commitment to the ideals of the institution (Rice and Austin 1988).

> *[Classic Hall] was very much a part of Hanover from so far back, and it stood for things forever important. It is a sorrow to bid farewell to a building where thousands of people have learned much about themselves and the world and God. But true loyalty to those things old Classic stood for makes*

us turn with abundant faith and pride to the new building
(Baker 1978, p. 195).

*A major disaster...struck [Luther College] when the Main
Building was gutted by fire May 19, 1889.... In September
1889, the committee voted to rebuild on the original site....
When the structure was rebuilt, the foundation and in large
part the walls of the old building were utilized.... A.K. Bai-
ley, representing Decorah, said in part: "Beautiful as are
all these surroundings, they are but a means to an end; they
constitute but a habitation in which is to reside the purpose—the soul—[that] is the real self of Luther College. The
shell was burned; the habitation was partly destroyed; but
the real college still survived because it was enshrined in
hearts that made it the subject of their hopes, their tears,
and their prayers"* (Nelson 1961, pp. 133–36).

Sometimes additions to the physical plant have been made in
an effort to change an institution's external image. Edward
Jennings, the president of Ohio State University in 1981,
attempted to alter the local image of the university as "a foot-
ball-playing school" by sponsoring a design competition for a
contemporary arts center to be constructed on the campus. The
competition received national press coverage and considerable
attention from the local media, thus garnering the desirable
publicity (Williams 1985).

At Indiana University, student housing was planned as carefully as academic buildings. Fraternity and sorority houses and
residence halls were constructed on the periphery of the campus, away from private dwellings; thus, students could cavort
and express their exuberance out of doors on warm spring and
fall evenings without disturbing the citizens of Bloomington
(Wells 1980).

Ceremonials, rites, and rituals
Ceremonials, rites, and rituals on a college campus give form
to communal life. They enrich the campus ethos and allow
interpretations and meanings to be made of special events. At
Amherst College, freshman convocation marked the formal
opening of the academic year. A description of the symbolic
rite of freshman induction illustrates how several artifactual
forms are blended to communicate important aspects of the institution's culture, such as roles, status, and expectations for
student and faculty behavior (Meister 1982):

[New students] were seated in the balcony of the college chapel, a spare but capacious and elegant example of nineteenth century congregational architecture. On the pale blue walls of the chapel hang the oil portraits of past college presidents as well as those of a few illustrious alumni like Calvin Coolidge...; while students file in, the pews on the main floor below remain empty. With...organ fanfare, the faculty marshall, who is the most senior member of the faculty, enters the chapel in full academic regalia, followed by the president and dean, and then by the body of the faculty in descending order of seniority. The untenured, new faculty bring up the rear.... The president welcomes both students and faculty. Honorary degrees are then conferred.... More music, and then the president delivers his convocation address, which is directed as much to faculty as to the students. Civility, tolerance, and vision are the themes. The faculty is complimented for its dedication and wisdom. More music...the organ recessional, the students remaining respectfully until the faculty have passed out of the chapel...(p. 33).

The chapel setting underscores the importance of conventional religion; the processional and convocation address emphasize that the faculty are the knowledge priests and students are novitiates who are there to learn (Meister 1982).

Lantern night at Bryn Mawr also was an initiation ceremony. For the first time, freshmen wore the cap and gown, the distinguishing marks of student status, and formed two semicircles between two residence halls, claiming the college buildings as their own:

Coming from Pembroke Arch, the sophomores [sang] Pallas Athene Thea *and pass[ed] the lanterns they carr[ied] to freshmen, symbolizing the light that illumined the way through college life. The freshmen then carried their lanterns through each college building, while the sophomores wait[ed] outside. At the return to Pembroke, all classes joined in cheers and sang the college hymn* (Horowitz 1984, p. 170).

The promise of community, however, was misleading. For the next 12 hours, Bryn Mawr freshmen had to protect their caps and gowns from the sophomores, who attempted to steal them so that the freshmen would not be appropriately dressed for chapel the next morning (Horowitz 1984).

This mock battle had an analogue on many campuses. At Wellesley, for example, sophomores tried to identify the freshman class song, class motto, and flower—all of which were to be kept secret until the public presentation at Tree Day. At Vassar, the process was reversed: Freshmen attempted to discover the time and place of the sophomore class tree dedication, which was to be a secret ceremony. Often sophomores would try to embarrass the freshmen by sending them out on false leads (Horowitz 1984).

Freshman induction ceremonies (and accompanying hazing practices) have been widespread. At Luther College, the freshmen could be accepted into the college community at one of two times: when they were able to retrieve a freshman beanie tacked on the top of a greased pole erected in the center of campus (which rarely occurred, as upperclassmen pelted freshmen with eggs and spoiled fruits); or during the half time of the homecoming football game later in the fall semester. Freshmen celebrated their acceptance into the college by tossing their beanies into the air.

At the Bloomington campus of Indiana University, the rite of freshman induction includes an oral description of the "spirit of Indiana," the charge to the class from the president (or designate), and a pledge to the university similar to the oath taken by free-born Athenian youth in ancient Greece (Wells 1980).

Similar rites and rituals also mark the departure of seniors on many campuses. "The final step singing, where seniors passed on their power to the class beneath them, the senior play, festive dinner, and finally commencement itself, celebrated the success of a graduating class and framed their transition to the world outside" (Horowitz 1984, pp. 173–74; see also Rice and Austin 1988). At Reed College, seniors celebrate the completion of their thesis with a parade. En masse, the seniors march from the library to the president's office to present the completed projects (Mitzman 1979). At many large universities, commencement is a weekend affair made up of several events that together become the celebration of the culmination of the baccalaureate experience.

Distinctive Themes

...The more we have learned about colleges, the more we have been struck by their uniqueness. True, colleges run to "types," and types ultimately converge on a national aca-

*demic model. One might therefore lump together the Univer-
sities of Massachusetts and Connecticut, or Harvard and
Yale, or Boston College and Fordham, or San Francisco
State and San Diego. But on closer inspection these colleges
appear to draw on quite different publics, and to have quite
different flavors* (Riesman and Jencks 1962, p. 132).

"Colleges profess to be, and often are, civilizing agencies;
they work to develop and refine the powers of intellect, perception, and feeling" (Clark and Trow 1966, p. 19); they intend
to "transmit culture, to bring about changes in the values and
beliefs with which students arrive" (Sanford 1962b, p. 59).
The extent to which a college is able to induce these civilizing
changes in the values and beliefs of students is evidence of its
potency (Astin 1985). Potency is the extent to which the campus norms, values, practices, and beliefs are rigidly enforced
and exert a marked influence over faculty and student behavior.
A college's potency is enhanced if its reputation is salient
(Clark 1960) and consistent with the institutional ethos, the
moral and esthetic aspects of the institution's culture. Under
these conditions, the institutional culture is both strong and salient, conditions required for distinctiveness. Antioch, Bennington, Haverford, Reed, and Swarthmore are institutions with
high image and campus potency (Clark et al. 1972; Newcomb
et al. 1967). The effects of attending a potent college are "con-
versionlike" or at least reinforcing; in this sense, conversion
refers to significant liberating changes in students' attitudes.
   Another factor that distinguishes one institution from others
is the degree to which the institution identifies with clearly defined external audiences and vice versa. In the 1950s, in the
early years of the expansion of community colleges, traditional
views of what a college should be (i.e., attract bright students
and faculty with credentials from prestigious graduate schools)
undermined the development of a salient image for the community college. The evolution from junior colleges to comprehensive community colleges helped foster a "folk halo [that]
encouraged acceptance of the two-year college by local citizens
as 'their college' " (Clark 1960, p. 173). Even so, when institutions have numerous broad purposes, "it is much more difficult to know specifically what the enterprise is about than in
specialized agencies. Even such widely accepted, secure public institutions as the American high school find themselves
plagued with the problem of identity" (p. 173).

Size is also a factor; in general, the larger the institution, the less potent its impact on students and the less distinctive the institution's image is likely to be. Large universities like the University of California–Berkeley, Ohio State University, and the University of Texas at Austin have complex purposes and multiple commitments—research, graduate education, preparation for a wide range of occupations, and service to business, industry, and government agencies. In a small liberal arts college, singularity of purpose is easier to attain and is reflected by a relatively uncomplicated administrative structure. Of course, an emphasis on undergraduate education alone does not guarantee quality. That is, a focus on general education at a baccalaureate-granting college cannot, by itself, compensate for a mediocre faculty or disinterested students. But when able students are met by motivated teacher-scholars, an institution with a coherent mission is more likely to develop stronger threads of continuity that lead to shared visions and actions (Clark 1970; Clark et al. 1972; Kuh 1981) and, in all likelihood, a distinctive institutional culture.

The Haverford experience is not distinctive necessarily because it is small, or has a well-known intellectual tradition, or attracts highly able students. Haverford's salient image is a function of these factors and other institutional features integrated within an atmosphere of value and belief congruent with the Friends' philosophy of life. Strong norms at Haverford discourage self-aggrandizement and status. First names are used in lieu of "Dr." or "President." To display a Phi Beta Kappa key has been considered ostentatious, and students have refused to accept such awards. Within the student body, little consciousness of social class traditionally has existed. Friendships cut across academic class and other artificial lines (Heath 1968). The honor system and other Quaker traditions have resulted in a practically nonexistent rate of academic dishonesty.

Fifth Day Meeting, a form of Friends' group worship, was a required, communal activity until 1966 and afforded an opportunity to discuss value-laden issues like the desegregation of local barber shops, the United States's involvement in Vietnam, and even criticism of the Meeting itself. These discussions embodied the most basic Quaker values: simplicity, respect, responsibility, loving acceptance, equality of individual work, and corporateness. The meaning of Meeting in the Haverford community was very subjective: "It was the one common experience of the entire intellectual community in which the *irrational* was accepted and valued" (Heath 1968, p. 46).

The Haverford ethos, based on the college's religious ethical tradition, demanded that students meet high standards in

> *...integrity, honesty, simplicity, and respect by other students and faculty...in* all *areas of their lives.... Intellectual tradition is obviously important [but] we fail to illuminate its integral relation to both the communal and religious-ethical tradition of the college* (Heath 1968, pp. 245–47).

Part of the unusual character of Swarthmore also is reflected in the subtleties of the Quaker influence. Unlike Haverford, though, Swarthmore moved from denominational control to an independent, secular liberal arts college. Yet Quakerism has continued to influence the campus climate.

> *Respect for inner conviction, low-key debate, the search for the unifying sense of the meeting—these sensitive and tolerant aspects of liberal Quaker thought were reflected in faculty meetings and administrative discussions. The tolerant religious morality put academic freedom beyond doubt. The Friends' commitment to social action was shared by enough members of the faculty to make itself felt by the students* ...(Clark et al. 1972, p. 36).

Individual Actors
Individuals often loom larger than life in the making of an organizational saga and sustaining a campus culture. Some have described the college president as the symbolic embodiment of the institution (Clark 1970, 1972; Kauffman 1980; Kerr and Gade 1984). For example, educated at Harvard and with faculty experience at Bowdoin, William T. Foster, the first president of Reed College, intended that Reed become a place "in which intellectual enthusiasm should be dominant" and where "student life would revolve around persistent and serious study...[with] uncompromising elimination" of diversions (Mitzman 1979, p. 39). A demanding curriculum was put into place. The student culture was characterized by "academic sobriety and intellectual intensity" (Mitzman 1979, p. 42). And through Foster's own form of public relations, "Reed became known as uniquely sensible and progressive, a place that went

its own way...but one worthy to stand among the finest colleges in the land" (Mitzman 1979, p. 40).

Miami-Dade College has been described as the best community college in the country (Roueche, cited in Zwerling 1988). Much of the credit is given to Miami-Dade's president, Robert McCabe, who took a risky, potentially volatile position by demanding that academic standards at the open-door institution be increased. At that time, at two of the four Miami-Dade campuses, the modal grade was an A. McCabe's attempt to reform the institution, which enrolls more students for whom English is a second language than any other institution in the world, was described as "the most comprehensive revision in modern higher education" (Zwerling 1988, p. 15). In one five-year period, 13,000 students were purportedly suspended because of insufficient academic performance. An "academic alert system" was developed to ensure that students in academic difficulty are forewarned through an individualized letter six weeks into every semester. The "advisement and graduation information system" was also established, permitting students to monitor their own progress toward meeting degree requirements. For these and many other accomplishments, McCabe has been described as "a model of leadership excellence worthy of emulation" (Roueche, cited in Zwerling 1988, p. 17).

Institutional agents in addition to presidents also can shape an institution's culture (Bernier 1987). At Wabash College, for example, Dean George Kendall became an integral character in the institution's saga. "A prepossessing man, tall and straight,...his baldness added to his stature in the eyes of students. Habitually composed and even stern looking, he frequently broke suddenly into a wide grin, which became famous at Wabash" (Trippet 1982, p. 125). Kendall was the principal architect of institutional policy and was also responsible for all student services. He did not believe in coddling students. In contrast to the numerous rules and petty prohibitions at most colleges, Wabash had only one rule of conduct: Students were to conduct themselves as gentlemen at all times, both on and off campus. (Bennington and Smith Colleges are other examples of institutions that did not initially develop arbitrary rules for student behavior—Horowitz 1984.) This philosophy predated by decades the demise of in loco parentis and became a distinctive thread in the institutional tapestry of the college. When the code was violated, Kendall responded quickly and firmly, using only one disciplinary measure when warranted: suspension from the college. Because Wabash students already enjoyed the freedoms that were being demanded elsewhere during the 60s, Wabash encountered only minor problems with the student unrest that plagued most campuses during that era (Trippet 1982).

Summary
Institutional culture is shaped by history, tradition, religious convictions of founders, and the attitudes of faculty, students, administrators, alumni, and others. Culture is carried and reflected by the academic program, social environment, and artifacts such as language, ceremonials, stories, and heroes. Architecture and other aspects of the physical environment also maintain and enrich an institution's culture. Individual institutional agents and benefactors can have a significant influence on culture. The institutional saga and stories often emphasize the role of presidents and other heroic figures in shaping lasting traditions and curricular aims.

Most of the examples of institutional culture in the literature are from small colleges. It does not necessarily imply, however, that distinctive or strong cultures can be found only at such institutions. Nevertheless, institutional size (e.g., number of students and faculty) seems to be an important factor in maintaining a coherent, distinctive culture.

INSTITUTIONAL SUBCULTURES

If we wish to discover where the cultural action lies in organizational life, we will probably have to discard some of our tacit (and not so tacit) presumptions about organizational culture and move to the group level of analysis. It is here where people discover, create, and use culture, and it is against this background that they judge the organization of which they are a part (Van Maanen and Barley 1984, p. 351).

The meanings people make of events and actions within a college or university are fragmented by a number of elements, including roles (e.g., student, faculty member, administrator), disciplines, and focus of interests (e.g., teaching, research, service). People who hold similar views on matters may be members of an institutional subculture (Van Maanen and Schein 1979).

This section describes three institutional subcultures that have received attention from scholars: faculty, students, and administrators. First, using Van Maanen and Barley's earlier definition (1985), it examines the subculture of the academic profession as a whole and the subcultures that reflect some of the subspecialties that make up the academy. Then, it describes and examines student subcultures, including their formation and their influence on student learning. Finally, it reviews the literature on administrative groups and considers whether it is appropriate to consider them as constituting an institutional subculture.

Segmentation and fragmentation are characteristic of the academic profession, but an integrating effect of overarching basic values also exists.

Faculty Subcultures

In the study of higher education, two perspectives on the academic subculture predominate (Metzger 1987). According to one view, academics make up a "single homogenous profession" (Becher 1987), characterized more by similarities than differences. The academic profession has also been described, however, as a complex of subprofessions (Bess 1982) or many professions (Ruscio 1987). According to this view, the basic trend in academic culture is fragmentation brought about by a proliferation of parts that operate under the centrifugal force of a growing number of differing needs and interests. In other words, the academic profession, as a monolithic subculture, does not exist (Light 1974).

The following sections examine whether the academic profession is best characterized as a single subculture or as a federation of discipline-based subcultures. They also examine subcultures within subcultures, including disciplinary subspecialties, and consider whether women faculty, ethnic and racial minority faculty, and part-time faculty are subcultures.

The academic profession as a subculture

The culture of the academic profession is based on the concepts and symbols of academic freedom, the community of scholars, scrutiny of accepted wisdom, truth seeking, collegial governance, individual autonomy, and service to society through the production of knowledge, the transmission of culture, and education of the young (Clark 1980; Morrill and Spees 1982; Ruscio 1987). The belief that a single academic profession and one academic culture exist is based on the assumption that all college and university faculty members share a common view of the world and scholarship. This world view is based on similar understandings about the nature and purposes of higher education and of colleges and universities, and the role of faculty within them (Bowen and Schuster 1986; Freedman 1979; Gusfield and Riesman 1968; Ruscio 1987).

The culture of the academic profession also provides a general identity for all faculty, regardless of disciplinary affiliation; "sweeping across all fields and institutions, assumed by professors of biology, sociology, and classics alike, is the identity of 'academic man' " (Clark 1984, p. 91). Components of this common identity include three basic values shared by faculty members across academic specialties and institutional types, deviations from which are resisted (Bowen and Schuster 1986).

The first basic value is the pursuit and dissemination of knowledge as the purpose of higher education. The primary responsibility of faculty members, then, is to be learned and to convey this learning by means of teaching, inquiry, and publication. The second basic value shared by faculty is autonomy in the conduct of academic work. Faculty members believe that freedom is necessary to advance learning and so have developed structures that reinforce autonomy: peer review, tenure, and relatively independent colleges and universities. The third shared value is collegiality, and it is demonstrated in a community of scholars that provides mutual support and opportunities for social interaction and in faculty governance. Thus, according to faculty members, an ideal academic community is a college or university in which the pursuit of learning, academic freedom, and collegiality are strongly held values.

Academic systems in colleges and universities have been described as "ideologically loaded" (Clark 1980, p. 1); "they work with the ideas of their particular discipline, they are self-defined critics of society, and they are likely to have a strong opinion about the proper purpose and shape of their own campuses" (Clark 1970, p. 253). These ideologies of the academic system portray faculty as people of ideas, sharing values of altruism, truth, and the life of the mind. In a scene from *The Small Room*, a group of faculty at a small college talk about what it means to be an academic:

> *But you are willing to grant, surely, that there is such a thing as a life of the mind?... It seems to me that we are talking round and round the same nub, and the nub is the "life of the mind" and how it is nourished or stimulated.... Are we not the way rather than the end? It is not our function to lead the honest mind necessarily to venture upon our path, but to find its own—and these paths must be different* (Sarton 1961, pp. 234–35).

Disciplinary subcultures
Some scholars assert that differences within the academic profession are more important and have greater impact than the similarities (Becher 1987). The commonalities, however—the shared picture of what a faculty member is and does—can obscure the underlying differences and their sources.

A study of the American professoriate found that faculty members in different disciplines exhibited different attitudes, values, and personal characteristics (Bowen and Schuster 1986). Significant differences among faculty members found across institutions were more closely related to discipline than to type of institution. For example, a study of political and academic attitudes found systematic differences among faculty grouped by discipline: The most liberal attitudes were expressed by faculty in the social sciences, the most conservative by faculty in the applied professional fields (Ladd and Lipset 1975–76).

The culture of the discipline is the primary source of faculty identity and expertise and typically engenders stronger bonds than those developed with the institution of employment, particularly in large universities. This case is increasingly evident as academic subject matter becomes increasingly narrow in focus, requiring more specialized training (Blau 1973; Clark 1984; Morrill and Spees 1982). Elements of the culture of the discipline include assumptions about what is to be known and how, assumptions about the tasks to be performed and standards for effective performance, and assumptions about patterns of publication, patterns of professional interaction, and social and political status (Becher 1984, 1987; Clark 1984).

"A discipline is the first mark of identity a professor receives" (Ruscio 1987, p. 332). Identification with a particular discipline is developed by means of socialization processes in graduate school and in the first faculty position (Bess 1982; Clark 1984; Freedman 1979). In these settings, a faculty member absorbs the canons of the specialty that provide a sense of belonging and define a disciplinary way of life and comes to understand the symbolic meanings of professional activities. In the words of a graduate student learning to become a faculty member:

> *In terms of research, academics has a creative tinge to it that allows people to adopt the artist's mode of existence. You know, we can be weird, as long as we're good, we can be weird. I don't think that happens in other parts of society. In academics you don't have to strive for that kind of power or wealth or fame in order to be able to do your thing quietly...* (Katz and Hartnett 1976, p. 138).

The novice must also become aware of and internalize the content and parameters of the discipline, including its language, its intellectual traditions and style, its folklore, and its patterns of relationships (Becher 1987). The following statement was made by a graduate student—and future faculty member—in biochemistry:

> *I think of people as biological organisms.... Studying neural chemistry has made me realize that life is flowing and beautiful and dancing on all levels. It contains all the energy—destructive, creative, and so on—on all levels, and so in a way you know, it's an affirmation of life and a teacher of a way of life* (Katz and Hartnett 1976, p. 135).

Disciplinary subcultures can be found in academic departments and in programs for professional education (Clark 1980; Millett 1962). In the latter case, disciplinary culture tends to reflect the norms and assumptions of the major occupational areas for which the school provides preparation as well as those of the graduate education experiences of faculty members. For example, faculty members in education are likely to focus their efforts toward improving educational practice in the "real world" of schools by means of consultation as well as research (Becher 1987).

Variations in disciplinary cultures tend to reflect variations in intellectual tasks among the disciplines (Becher 1984, 1987). For example, the nature of knowledge within the pure sciences is cumulative and concerned with simplification and universals, resulting in explanation or discovery. In turn, elements of disciplinary culture in the pure sciences include competition, teamwork, rapid rates of publication, and effective political organization (Becher 1987). Physics, for example, is characterized by strong consensus about problems to be addressed and how to address them; findings usually build on one another in a linear fashion. In addition, because high-cost areas of inquiry are involved, physicists have found that it is in their collective interest to speak with one voice about their needed resources (Becher 1987). Thus, the disciplinary culture of physics is typically tightly coupled around political and economic goals as well as assumptions about knowledge and research.

Disciplinary cultures are also affected by their institutional context, as "faculty subcultures have institutional as well as disciplinary foundations" (Ruscio 1987, p. 353). Different sectors of higher education have developed different missions to meet the needs of different segments of the postsecondary market (Clark 1963; Ruscio 1987). Community colleges have typically included community development and adult education in their missions. Liberal arts colleges are usually committed to high-quality teaching of undergraduates and education of "the whole person."

Differences in mission and commitment in turn affect the recruitment, socialization, tasks, and performance standards of faculty members (Clark 1963; Ruscio 1987). For example, a faculty member in a liberal arts college is likely to have a heavy teaching load, work primarily with undergraduates who have relatively shallow knowledge of the subject area, be part of a small department that lacks colleagues of similar special interests, and have opportunities to collaborate with colleagues in different disciplines. In this case, the faculty member's role in and commitment to the institution may interfere with her or his involvement in and commitment to the discipline (Blau 1973; Caplow and McGee 1968).

Institutional size and complexity are also likely to affect disciplinary subcultures (Clark 1963, 1984). Larger and more complex colleges and universities are more likely to have numerous faculty subcultures than a unified faculty culture; "the subgroups are not duplicate cells, or units split on a single criterion, but are unlike cells, established by multiple criteria" (Clark 1963, p. 139). Thus, in addition to divisions along disciplinary lines, one may find subcultures based on length of service (e.g., junior faculty groups), commitment to collective bargaining (e.g., union versus nonunion groups), contract type (e.g., part-time faculty groups), involvement with student activities, and so on (Ruscio 1987). These groups can be considered subcultures, however, only if they have persistent interaction and mechanisms for socialization and social control (Van Maanen and Barley 1985).

The administrative structures of institutions also shape faculty subcultures. For example, institutions of a "management temperament" can be distinguished from those of an "academic temperament" (Ruscio 1987, p. 355). The former type is characterized by decision making and constraints on actions set "on high" (Ruscio 1987, p. 355) by administrators who have a broad vision for the institution across departments and disciplines. This arrangement may be typical of those institutions in which administrators have longer service than faculty or in which faculty subcultures are weak or not committed to involvement in institutional decision making. In institutions of an academic temperament, the tone for decisions and governance is "set from below" (Ruscio 1987, p. 353) by faculty members within departments and disciplines. Disciplinary subcultures are likely to be particularly strong in this type of institution, although faculty may also be divided by political positions and influence.

Membership in a discipline is affirmed by interaction with local and national colleagues (Clark 1980). These "invisible colleges" (Becher 1987, p. 286) of colleagues encourage contacts and cooperation among members and reaffirm the values of the discipline with regard to appropriate research problems and methods, appropriate interactions among colleagues, and desirable patterns of publication. Professional associations also provide a powerful sense of disciplinary identity by reinforcing networks of collegial support and disciplinary values by means of admissions requirements, mission statements, association publications and conferences, and awards (Clark 1980).

A number of classification systems have been developed for the study of academic disciplines. These systems employ different classification criteria, including epistemology (Becher 1987; Snow 1959), development of paradigms (Lodahl and Gordon 1972), personality archetypes (Mitroff and Kilmann 1978), and status of knowledge (Parsons and Platt 1973).

One of the best-known typologies of disciplinary culture was developed by Clark (1963, 1980), who expanded the local-cosmopolitan characterization developed by Gouldner (1957) to provide a more detailed description of higher education faculty. Clark identified three dimensions of faculty orientations: (1) local-cosmopolitan, based on orientation to the institution and orientation to the discipline; (2) pure-applied, based on orientation to use of knowledge; and (3) humanistic-scientific, based on commitment to personal interpretation or public verification of knowledge. The interactions of these dimensions produce four groups of faculty members: (1) the teacher (high identification with institution, high commitment to pure study); (2) the scholar-researcher (low institutional identification, high commitment to pure study); (3) the demonstrator (high institutional identification, low commitment to pure study); and (4) the consultant (low institutional identification, low commitment to pure study) (Clark 1963).

A three-dimensional model of academic disciplines includes (1) hard-soft, based on presence or absence of consensus on a body of theory; (2) pure-applied, based on presence or absence of concern for applications to practical problems; and (3) life-nonlife, based on the presence or absence of a research focus on living systems (Biglan 1973). Research on this model has tended to confirm that faculty members differing along these three dimensions also differ in their professional goals, tasks, and satisfaction (Creswell and Bean 1981).

Becher's classification (1987) of four disciplinary groups is based on the nature of knowledge within the discipline. The first discipline, "hard-pure" or pure sciences, is characterized by cumulative and atomistic knowledge and concern for universals, simplification, and discovery. The second group, "soft-pure" or humanities and social sciences, is concerned with particulars, understanding, and holistic and reiterative knowledge. The third group, "hard-applied" or technologies (e.g., mechanical engineering), emphasizes products, techniques, and pragmatic and purposive knowledge. Finally, the fourth group, "soft-applied" or applied social sciences (e.g., education), is concerned with the enhancement of professional practice and utilitarian knowledge.

Whether these various typologies describe subcultures is questionable. The authors' criteria for a subculture include regular interaction, group self-consciousness, shared problems, and action based on distinct collective understandings (Van Maanen and Barley 1985). According to these criteria, the classifications set forth by Clark, Biglan, Becher, and others do not describe subcultures but, rather, role orientations or ideal types. To the extent, however, that similar role orientations create opportunities for interaction, they may provide a basis for the development of disciplinary subcultures among faculty.

Differential interaction among an organization's membership may reflect physical proximity, the sharing of common tasks or status,...or even accidents of history.... To the degree that some members interact more frequently with others who share similar problems, this is where the seeds of organizational subcultures are sown (Van Maanen and Barley 1985, p. 37).

Thus, faculty members in history, who share a strong identification with their discipline and common assumptions about the nature of knowledge, may be more likely to interact with one another and thereby create conditions for the development of a subculture than faculty members in history who strongly identify with their institution. The disciplines themselves, however, can also be divided by subspecialty, gender, race, and contract status.

Subcultures within academic subcultures
Each discipline comprises a number of separate areas of inquiry, or specialties. The specialties obtain strong loyalties from the faculty within them; "to affiliate with a particular specialism [sic] is to become, except in a few heavily populated areas, a member of a relatively small and close-knit community" (Becher 1987, p. 292). In most cases, members of specialties are a reference group for ideas and professional support and have fairly regular contact with one another.

In the past two decades, other groups have emerged within the faculty that may or may not be considered subcultures. These groups include women faculty, minority faculty, and part-time faculty (Bowen and Schuster 1986). Consider just one of them: women. Sociolinguistic research (Philips 1980) suggests that the language of men and women is quite different. For example, the language of women is more inclusive; women are likely to use questions as part of a general strategy to continue conversations, to seek connections between themes in the discussion (Mitchell 1987), and to elicit the ideas and feelings of others (Gilligan 1982). Men use questions as simple requests for information and to establish a hierarchy of issues. Men and women have different styles of communication and often fail to perceive the other's style because of differences in topic shifts, self-disclosure, aggressiveness, interruption, and listening (Coates 1986). The analysis of language patterns of men and women administrators suggests a clashing of two cultures. Thus, the possibility for gender-specific subcultures has some theoretical and empirical support.

Whether any one of the groups listed above (women, minorities, part-time faculty) is a subculture depends on the definition of subculture one chooses. If a subculture is a group of people with common problems (cf. Schein 1985; Van Maanen and Schein 1979), then women, minority, and part-time faculty may be subcultures within disciplinary and academic cultures. Shared problems may also lead to interactions that, if continued, could lead to the development of subcultures (Van Maanen and Barley 1985). If, however, a subculture is a group of people who have persistent interaction, a distinct group identity, and collective distinct understandings that form the basis for action, women, minority, and part-time faculty would not typically be considered subcultures.

Conclusion

Is the academic profession one subculture or many subcultures? The answer, it seems, is "yes"—or, rather, "both." Segmentation and fragmentation are characteristic of the academic profession, but an integrating effect of overarching basic values also exists (Ruscio 1987).

Paradoxically, the more it becomes possible to portray the components of the academic world as fragmented and particularized, and the more readily it can be shown that these components are in a constant state of change, the more one is inclined to apprehend that world in its entirety.... By understanding the parts and acknowledging their particularity,

one can better understand the whole,...e pluribus unum
(Becher 1987, p. 298).

Student Cultures
A student's peer group exerts significant influence over the
quality of the college experience (Bushnell 1962). Students' interactions with peers, with faculty, and with institutional structures and processes are likely to lead to the development of
some kind (or kinds) of student culture (Hughes, Becker, and
Geer 1962), which is defined as:

> *...a whole body of conceptions and images of problems and
> situations and of proper and justifiable solutions of them ar-
> rived at by the students; in part passed along from one gen-
> eration of students to another, in part apparently rediscov-
> ered—or at least reinforced—by each succeeding generation
> as they pass through the same experiences* (Hughes, Becker,
> and Geer 1962, p. 518).

Another definition holds that student culture:

> *...consists of the taken-for-granted patterns of eating, sleep-
> ing, socializing; the embraced and disgraced habits of study;
> the rules of thumb about what activities on campus count as
> status enhancing or status degrading; the norms surrounding
> what is proper demeanor in and out of the classroom; the
> loose consensus among students as to what classes are
> "gut" and what are not; the grapevine gossip that tells stu-
> dents those teachers to take and those to avoid.... In brief,
> student cultures offer their members thick and thin guidelines
> for how to get an education and thus define for students just
> what an education means* (Van Maanen 1987, p. 5).

These descriptions imply the existence of a dominant student
culture, a set of beliefs, attitudes, and values shared by all (or
most) students in a particular institution. The dominant student
culture may reflect or refute the central ideals of the institution
as a whole. Thus, it is another powerful influence on an institution's culture:

> *Students...are free to form their own structures and to bring
> their own values to bear on the rest of the institution. Stu-
> dents can change their majors as well as their courses, vot-*

ing with their physical presence for and against different professors, courses, programs, and departments. They can alter the intensity of their participation, seeking to move closer to a professor or to flee contact.... And they have the ultimate step..., dropping out altogether and transferring to another place. Most important is that they come with personal inclinations and then informally relate to one another in patterns that uphold the predispositions or alter them. As a result...the student body becomes a major force in defining the institution (Clark 1970, pp. 252–53).

Thus, any effort to change traditional practices must take into account the dominant student culture and attempt to obtain students' support for any proposed change(s). In this sense, the student culture can become a conservative force, steadfastly protecting the status quo (Clark 1970). This perspective is different from that suggested by the legacy of the 1960s—that students are more likely than other groups in a college or university to press for change.

A historical review of undergraduate life in the United States identifies three dominant student cultures, two of which emerged in the late eighteenth century (Horowitz 1987). The first of these cultures was "college life," or "the culture of the college man" (Horowitz 1987, p. 12). The elements of college life included insubordination (particularly toward faculty), hedonism, minimal academic effort, an emphasis on social skills and fair play, athletic prowess, and solidarity with others in the group.

To an important degree, the college world they made was their reading of the present so that they might claim it for their future. To those heading for the combat of American capitalism, the trials of the extracurriculum appeared to offer valuable lessons (p. 12).

The culture of college life was also adaptable. At the beginning of the twentieth century, faculty and administration gave leaders of the culture of college life power to serve as official leaders of the student body as a whole. Thus, the focus of the culture shifted from a position of hostility toward authority to cooperation. The addition of women to the university campus also added the element of dating "the right girl" to the prestige structure of the culture of the college male. Women students

Any effort to change traditional practices must take into account the dominant student culture and attempt to obtain students' support for any proposed change(s).

at coeducational institutions formed a "college life" culture equivalent to that of the men, although the focus of the female culture was "college as a way station to a proper marriage" (Horowitz 1987, p. 200).

The second student culture was the "outsiders." The original outsiders—those of the eighteenth century—were future ministers who tried to avoid the hedonism of "college life"; college was a time to prepare for a vocation, not for fun. From the middle of the nineteenth century until the middle of the twentieth, American colleges and universities welcomed an influx of new outsiders, including farm youth, women, immigrants, blacks, World War II veterans, commuters, and returning women. The primary focus of these students was hard work in college as a means to future success, and they regarded faculty as mentors and allies (Horowitz 1987).

The third student culture, "the rebels," emerged in the early twentieth century to express opposition to "college life" (Horowitz 1987); "college rebels fought the social distinctions that sorted out college students and reveled in difference, not uniformity" (p. 16). Rebels were, for the most part, students whose backgrounds (especially Judaism) kept them out of "college life," although their interests combined the academic orientation of the "outsiders" with the hedonism of the "college man." The 1930s have been described as the period of ascendancy of the college rebels because they were extremely active and visible in support for unionization, civil liberties, and peace and in opposition to fascism, privilege, and anti-immigration movements (Horowitz 1987).

Formation of student subcultures

Student subcultures represent different group responses to problems faced by all students at the same institution (Bolton and Kammeyer 1972; Hughes, Becker, and Geer 1962)—how to succeed academically, how to make friends, how to affect organizations and people. The formation of student subcultures is affected by characteristics of both organizations and students.

Influential student characteristics include precollege characteristics and acquaintance, propinquity (of residence, classes, organizational involvement), and similarity of attitudes, values, interests, and problems (Bushnell 1962; Newcomb 1962). "Undergraduates bring to their higher education a great deal of baggage from their short pasts" (Horowitz 1987, p. 11). That is, affiliations sought in college are affected by students' educational background, socioeconomic status, political and religious beliefs, goals for the college experience, and psychological characteristics and needs. Students who live near one another or attend class together or are isolated from nonstudents are more likely to meet and have opportunities for reciprocal exploration. Continuous interaction within an isolated group produces understandings and attitudes known as student culture (Hughes, Becker, and Geer 1962). These understandings include values (e.g., what to learn and how), aspirations and goals (e.g., career plans), and assumptions about appropriate social interaction. Students seek other students who think, or study, or party (or don't party) as they do; living down the corridor in a residence hall or sitting across the aisle in class facilitates finding one another.

Student subcultures are maintained through ceremonies and rituals (e.g., initiation of pledges, orientation of freshmen) and formal and informal mechanisms of social control (e.g., grade point requirements for membership, unwritten dress codes) (Bushnell 1962; Leemon 1972; Newcomb 1962). Formal and informal socialization processes are also important for the preservation of strong and cohesive student subcultures; in this way, values and behavioral norms are handed down, with some changes, from one student generation to the next (Bushnell 1962). For example, Greek organizations use pledge training programs to inform new members of the traditions and expectations of the group (Leemon 1972). Less formal socialization occurs through the "we've always done it this way" statements made by floor officers to freshmen residents with new ideas; "always," of course, can mean one or two years in the life of a student group.

The influence of the group on members is affected by the group's size (small enough for interaction), homogeneity of qualities likely to make for common attitudes (e.g., age, sex, socioeconomic status, religious affiliation), and the extent to which group members receive support from one another (Newcomb 1962). As shared understandings, interests, and problems change, the group may or may not stay together, depending on whether new common interests replace the old and whether group members maintain favorable attitudes toward one another (Newcomb 1962). Students bound by the need for support while negotiating freshman hurdles may find that sophomore year brings new challenges—selecting a major, reconsidering the need for a college degree—that the existing group may or may not be able to mediate.

The formation, maintenance, and potency of student subcultures are affected to a large extent by their institutional context (Becker, Geer, and Hughes 1968). Contextual factors that affect student cultures include the institutional ethos, interests of persons within the institution, authority structure, and institutional size and complexity (Clark and Trow 1966).

The institution's ethos includes its "official culture, historically derived" (Clark and Trow 1966, p. 32) and reflected in current beliefs and practices, organizational purposes, and institutional character. The more distinctive the institutional ethos, the more likely it will be that constraints will be placed on student cultures. For example, at Swarthmore in the 1920s, President Aydelotte's commitment to "intellectual distinction, English style" (Clark 1970, p. 185) demanded dramatic changes not only in the social life of students but also in the expectations students had for their entire college experience.

Faculty and administrators typically serve as the "donor society" from which the culture of the institution is transmitted to students, "the subordinate group" (Bushnell 1962, p. 511). The content of culture transmitted is usually oriented toward the intellectual tasks of the academy. At the same time, students are not simply passive recipients; they choose what cultural elements to adapt to and may use cultural elements in a manner not intended by the officials of the college. Commencement ceremonies in the 1960s became political platforms as students wore black armbands and used valedictory addresses to protest the Vietnam War. More recently, students at some institutions have turned commencement ceremonies into parties, complete with champagne.

The institution's authority structure provides support for its values and interests (Clark and Trow 1966). The extent to which students are involved in institutional governance may affect the nature of student cultures; lack of meaningful involvement may encourage a dominant student culture that is in conflict with institutional priorities. The student demonstrations of the late 1960s were, among other things, evidence of feelings of powerlessness to affect policy by means of normal channels of change (Horowitz 1987).

Large universities may hinder the interaction necessary for development of student cultures (Clark and Trow 1966). The effects of size, however, may be mediated by substructures based on homogenous interests and/or circumstances, such as living-learning housing units, fraternities and sororities, and commuter clubs, thereby encouraging development of multiple student cultures.

"The demands made by colleges on their client participants also shape the strength of the several subcultures. What does it take to get in, survive, and get out in good standing?" (Clark and Trow 1966, p. 58). High selectivity can contribute to the development of academically oriented subcultures. Rigorous performance standards may discourage participation in traditional collegiate subcultures. Consider the plight of a freshman at the University of Michigan:

> *"I'm having no fun."... All he heard around him was GPA—grade point average: "three letters I'm tired of hearing." He mimicked what he disliked: "Why should I mess up my GPA?" He had come to college because he saw it as a chance "to get away, to find yourself." But college had turned into "study, study, study." With everyone thinking about grades, he felt cheated: "You don't have time to expand"* (Horowitz 1987, p. 3).

Potency of student subcultures
Student subcultures offer means to cope with the difficulties of college life by providing students with social support and guidelines to live by (Hughes, Becker, and Geer 1962). Students learn to interpret events and problems according to attitudes and values present in the student subculture, "a perspective from which students can build consistent patterns of response, enabling them to fit into the activities of the school" (Hughes, Becker, and Geer 1962, p. 529).

Student subcultures also have consequences for the institutions in which they exist. Cultural understandings provide students with a rationale for what is to be learned, and how, and for the amount of effort to be expended on curricular and extracurricular activities, guidelines and expectations for relationships with faculty and administration and other students, and a basis for adjustment to and satisfaction with the college experience (Bushnell 1962; Hughes, Becker, and Geer 1962).

Descriptions of student subcultures
Descriptions of student subcultures have taken several forms, including case studies (Becker, Geer, and Hughes 1968; Becker

et al. 1961; Heath 1981; Leemon 1972; Scott 1965; Wallace 1966), historical reviews (Fass 1977; Horowitz 1984, 1987), and typologies (Clark and Trow 1966; Katchadourian and Boli 1985). Clark and Trow's typology of student subcultures (1966), perhaps the most well-known and the most controversial of these descriptions, posits four student subcultures: the collegiate culture, the vocational culture, the academic culture, and the nonconformist culture.

The collegiate subculture is "the most widely held stereotype of college life...a world of football, fraternities and sororities, dates, cars, drinking, and campus fun" (Clark and Trow 1966, p. 20). The values and activities of the collegiate subculture reflect loyalty to the college as an institution but disassociation from academic demands beyond the minimum necessary to obtain a diploma. This culture thrives on but is not limited to residential campuses.

For student members of the vocational subculture, college is a place to obtain job training and a diploma that will enable them to get a better job than they could otherwise. These students have little attachment to the college but, like members of the collegiate subculture, they are resistant to academic demands beyond what is required (Clark and Trow 1966).

The values of the academic subculture include identification with the intellectual priorities of faculty members, hard work, high grades, immersion in ideas and knowledge, and discussion of academic issues outside of class. If these values represent those of the college as a whole, then the academic student culture identifies with the college (Clark and Trow 1966).

The student nonconformist subculture is characterized by detachment from the college and faculty and general hostility to the administration. These students tend to use social and intellectual trends and off-campus groups as points of reference. The nonconformist subculture offers an alternative to the rebellious student who seeks a distinctive identity consistent with his or her experiences and personality (Clark and Trow 1966).

Whether or not these groups are in fact subcultures is debatable. Bolton and Kammeyer (1972) asserted that Clark and Trow had described students' general orientations but that the resulting groups did not meet criteria for subcultures, including persistent interaction, processes of socialization, mechanisms for social control, and norms that differed from the parent culture. Horowitz (1987) concluded that only the collegiate and the nonconformist groups were subcultures; the norms and beliefs of the academic and vocational groups were consistent with the culture of higher education in general and, so, were not distinct subcultures. Warren (1968) criticized the Clark-Trow typology for its ambiguity as well as its inflexibility; "the use of discrete categories to describe students does not allow for variation in degree [for those] who are weakly or strongly committed to the kind of attitudes and behavior that distinguish a particular subculture" (p. 214).

The same criticisms can be leveled at the typology of student cultures produced from a longitudinal study of Stanford University students (Katchadourian and Boli 1985), which identifies four categories of students on the basis of academic orientation: (1) careerists, for whom college is primarily a means to prepare for a vocation; (2) intellectuals, for whom college is a place to broaden academic interests and develop intellectual capacities; (3) strivers, who value both a liberal education and career preparation; and (4) the unconnected, who for no apparent reason remain detached from their college education. These groups also fail to qualify as subcultures according to the criteria of Van Maanen and Barley (1985) and Bolton and Kammeyer (1972).

Another researcher examined social fraternities and sororities at one university and concluded that these groups did constitute a student subculture (Scott 1965). Members of Greek organizations had constant contact with one another, the members' strong loyalty to the group made them susceptible to group influence, a clear distinction could be made between members and nonmembers, and group members shared values and definitions of right and wrong that could be used as consistent standards for judging actions. Greeks operate with a great deal of external control in the form of university rules and policies, however. As a consequence, "all of their processes, from recruitment through socialization to elimination, are performed with an eye to their cultural surroundings" (Scott 1965, p. 90). Greeks, therefore, exhibit congruence with the values of the dominant culture (Scott 1965) and so may not be subcultures as defined by Bolton and Kammeyer (1972) and Horowitz (1987).

Conclusion

In entering college, freshmen step into a complex environment containing alternative student cultures, each with its own standards and values. These particular undergraduate worlds give form to students' lives and meaning to their experience (Horowitz 1986, p. 1).

Student cultures affect students' perceptions of their work and social lives in college and their professional and personal goals for the future. Student cultures also affect the climate and culture of their institutional contexts and in turn the experience of all participants in higher education.

Administrative Subcultures
"Least noticed in the subcultures of academic enterprises and systems but of growing importance is the separation of administrative cultures from those of faculty and students" (Clark 1984, p. 89). As colleges and universities became increasingly complex and faculty members attempted to engage in all three traditional activities (teaching, research, and service), a separate group of academic workers emerged to handle the management of colleges and universities (Clark 1980; Millett 1962). Administrative positions run the gamut from president to residence hall director. General administrative functions include providing educational leadership, articulating and representing institutional priorities and values to internal and external audiences, acquiring and allocating resources, managing fiscal concerns, administering student services, and maintaining links among students, faculty, and all levels of administration (Austin and Gamson 1983; Millett 1962).

Except in the case of academic deans and department chairs, administrators tend not to come from the faculty, have training for their jobs that is very different from that of faculty members, have different interests and duties from faculty members, and interact with one another more than they interact with faculty (Clark 1980; Scott 1978). Thus, "a separate culture is generated" (Clark 1984, p. 89). The separateness of the administrative culture is enhanced as students and faculty perceive it as "distinct and even alien" (Clark 1984, p. 90) in its commitments, priorities, values, and assumptions. Administrators also associate with other administrators through national organizations that encourage the development of a professional identity separate from that of faculty and development of special areas of administrative expertise (Lunsford 1970).

Little empirical work has been published using cultural perspectives on administration. What is available suggests that higher education administrators are too diverse in duties and fragmented in location to constitute an institutional subculture. Task-related administrative groups, however (e.g., academic administrators, student affairs administrators, financial managers, physical plant staff), seem to fit Van Maanen and Barley's criteria for subcultures (1985): regular interaction both on and off campus; striving for group self-consciousness, especially at the national level; shared problems in performing their duties (e.g., communicating with students, faculty, and external audiences, allocating resources, and managing personnel); action on the basis of collective understandings (e.g., a bureaucratic perspective of colleges and universities; a commitment to student development; and a commitment to efficient management (Austin and Gamson 1983).

Summary

The cultures of colleges and universities are subdivided, complicated, and enriched by the development of subcultures around common roles, tasks, and problems. Groups of students, faculty, and administrators develop common beliefs, values, solutions, and norms as well as systems of symbols, rituals, and socialization processes to maintain their groups. Although higher education research has tended to focus on faculty groups and disciplinary subcultures,

> *[in] the conglomeration that we call a university, subcultures are bound to develop on grounds other than disciplinary location...[and] as the enterprise grows, subculturing around such major roles grows apace, setting student, faculty, and administrative worlds farther apart and developing further differences within each* (Clark 1984, p. 87).

Despite the significance of subcultures for understanding colleges and their cultures, the higher education literature contains little research grounded in a precise definition of subcultures. Extant typologies and other classification schemes purporting to identify subcultures tend rather to describe role orientations and ideal types.

IMPLICATIONS OF CULTURAL PERSPECTIVES

This section presents some implications of cultural perspectives for administrators, faculty, and scholars of higher education, briefly summarizing properties of institutional culture to provide a backdrop for the discussion of implications, discussing the feasibility of intentional efforts to change culture and describing the culture audit as a method for identifying cultural elements that influence actions and events in a college or university, and suggesting some ways to study and implications for studying culture in colleges and universities.

Culture is a holistic, context-bound, and subjective set of attitudes, values, assumptions, and beliefs.

A Summary of Cultural Properties

Culture is a holistic, context-bound, and subjective set of attitudes, values, assumptions, and beliefs. The meaning of events and actions cannot be interpreted out of the institutional context in which the events and actions take place. Behavior that seems to be effective in one institution may or may not be effective in another; what appear to be similar actions and events will mean different things in different settings. What people attend to and how they interpret actions and events are filtered through lenses colored by past experiences, current circumstances, and personal agendas (Lincoln 1985; Schwartz and Ogilvy 1979; Weick 1979). Much of what constitutes culture exists beneath conscious thought; that is, culture subtly shapes the "realities" perceived by individuals and groups. In effect, each person constructs reality for him or herself. Therefore, multiple realities exist, subjectivity is valid, and the illusion of a single objective reality that permeates conventional models of organizing is eschewed—which is not to say behavior cannot be understood. It can, but interpretations are context bound and person specific, generated by individuals making sense of what they observe and experience. Thus, managerial control of culture and the extent to which cultural properties can be changed intentionally are more limited than some have suggested. More about this point later.

Culture can be a stabilizing influence, providing a sense of continuity and a consistent framework within which behavior can be interpreted. Traditions, expectations, and routine practices are used to socialize new students and faculty into the norms and values of the institution. By connecting institutional stake holders to the institution's past, present, and future, culture militates against, or engenders, the development of commitment, loyalty, and cohesiveness. In this sense, culture can be either a barrier to developing a sense of community or may serve as the glue that binds an institution. At the same time, culture constantly evolves as it is shaped by the interaction of newcomers and culture bearers (e.g., junior and senior faculty) within the institution as well as by changes in the external environment. Culture can also be a divisive influence. Some aspects of student subcultures (e.g., racist behavior on the part of white students toward students of color) and faculty subcultures (e.g., loyalty to the discipline rather than to the institution) can thwart attainment of institutional purposes as well as denigrate the integrity of individuals.

Culture is revealed by examining artifacts like products (e.g., policies) and processes (e.g., decision making) and the values and assumptions on which products and processes are based. The relationships among cultural properties are complicated and difficult to describe and understand. The multiple, overlapping layers of culture (e.g., culture of society, culture of the region of the country, culture of the institution, culture of faculty discipline and student groups) make determining where one layer of culture ends and another begins virtually impossible. Some properties can even be paradoxical. For example, culture is both something a college or university *is* and something a college or university *has*. In addition, efforts to understand culture as a holistic influence on behavior often involve analysis of specific elements of culture (e.g., language, stories, values). Dividing culture into discrete elements violates the holistic nature of cultural phenomena, however, and makes it difficult to appreciate the pervasive shaping influence of an institution's culture.

The following implications are stated simply. We will, with good reason, be criticized for simplifying such inherently complicated properties. But "it's more complicated than that" (Berelson and Steiner 1964, cited in Weick 1980). Understanding institutional cultures is indeed more complicated than what follows might suggest.

Implications for Practice

1. *To understand and appreciate the distinctive aspects of a college or university, examine its culture.*

The practices, procedures, customs, and rituals of a college or university provide useful information about beliefs, values, and assumptions held by institutional agents. Cultural lenses provide an interpretive framework within which special events (e.g., Founders Day, homecoming) have particular significance and commonplace behaviors take on richer meaning. To appreciate the nuances of behavior in a college or university, an understanding and appreciation of the cultural milieu is necessary. Because culture is a complex set of properties and processes, the challenges to those using cultural perspectives cannot be overstated.

2. Cultural understanding is increased by focusing on the assumptions that form the basis of routine processes, such as decision making.

Individuals and groups rely on tacit, context-bound assumptions to interpret and judge events and actions. Faculty, students, parents, and others may use different assumptions to construe meaning in the institutional context; thus, multiple, often competing, systems of knowledge and understanding may exist (Kramer 1986). What people say (espoused values) and what they do (enacted values) are not always congruent. Assume and expect that people see different things and interpret differently what takes place. By carefully listening to what people say, the familiar may become strange. Clear expectations (e.g., expectations for promotion and tenure, appropriate amount of competition for grades) clarify a group's espoused values and make the values easier to talk about—although not necessarily easier to attain.

The assumptions at the core of an institution's culture influence daily activities as well as special events. Indeed, tacit assumptions and beliefs undergird many routine practices—for example, because undergraduate students are not considered mature and responsible, tuition bills and grade reports are sent to parents or guardians. What cultural assumptions are reflected by the annual performance review for faculty and staff or the new student admissions process (Kramer 1986)? What assumptions about human behavior and teaching and learning guide evaluation or grading practices? What artifacts (events, symbols, traditions, language) are important to faculty governance? (Tierney 1983).

Identifying hidden assumptions is difficult but not impossible. The culture audit, a systematic approach for becoming aware of cultural properties, including assumptions, is discussed later.

3. Groups of faculty and students share values and perspectives that differ, sometimes in significant ways, from the dominant institutional culture.

Colleges and universities, particularly large ones, can accommodate many subcultures. On balance, faculty and student subcultures are not necessarily problematic, as they offer a normative frame of reference with which certain people can identify and permit different behaviors to be rewarded (Deal and Kennedy 1982; Fetterman 1987). At the same time, the presence of subcultures with sharply contrasting views works against a feeling of community, dilutes the potency of the learning experience for students, and strains structures of campus governance.

4. An institution's ethos integrates history, tradition, values, ecological context, and individual personalities into an invisible tapestry or cultural web.

To understand institutional culture, one must understand and appreciate the institution's ethos, including the affective dimensions of the organization, such as loyalty, commitment, and even love (Trippet 1982). To preserve and enhance the unifying power of the ethos, social ties across constituent groups (alumni, faculty, students, parents) must be maintained to sustain common belief systems.

5. Managing meaning is an important responsibility of leaders.

People give meaning to institutional life through sense making, an interpretive process that forms the basis for understanding behavior, events, and actions (Boje, Fedor, and Rowland 1982; Weick 1979). Inventing symbols and helping people determine the meaning of the symbols and other cultural properties are important responsibilities of administrators and faculty leaders. "Important tools in the management of meaning include the nurturance of myth, the identification of unifying symbols, the ritual observance of symbols, the canonization of exemplars..." (Dill 1982, p. 316).

Administrators and faculty leaders can start by identifying important institutional symbols and the meanings various groups (e.g., faculty, student subcultures) give to these symbols. What symbols are invoked by faculty to demonstrate the relationship between teaching and research? What symbols characterize the character of the out-of-class life of students? How did these symbols come to be important to the institution and to the subcultures? Leaders must carefully consider the timing and the manner in which symbols are used in an effort to stir the consciousness, emotions, energies, and loyalties of others (Bredeson 1987). A leader's use of symbols may be judged as hollow unless his or her messages and actions are consistent and congruent with the meanings various groups usually attach to the symbol.

Leaders must be knowledgeable about the institution's history and translate stories and episodes from the institutional saga so that these artifacts speak to current exigencies. What information (history, saga) would be helpful in understanding how we got to where we are today? If a written history through the present does not exist, one should be produced so that a permanent record is made of the institution's past.

Administrators may encounter difficulty in mobilizing faculty and students to pursue goals that conflict with the institution's culture. Thus, what leaders do to articulate and act on their visions must be congruent with history, traditions, and nuances of language that flow from the institution's cultural context. Leaders must traffic in images (Weick 1985) that influence priorities, affirm values, clarify beliefs, reinforce or challenge behavioral norms, enthuse others, and garner resources.

As a consequence of the rapidly changing external context, the logic and strategies used by the institution in the past may no longer be functional. At such points, a crisis in meaning may occur (Dill 1982). Alternative images and a different language may be needed to explain the changing relationships between the institution, its constituents, and external agencies. Reinterpreting myths and presenting new symbols may stimulate development of new meanings. The term "turnaround saga" has been used to describe colleges (e.g., Simpson College in Iowa) that, like the mythical Phoenix, overcame adversity and are now moving forward (Rice and Austin 1988).

6. A core group of institutional leaders (e.g., senior faculty) provides continuity, which is integral to maintaining a cohesive institutional culture.

Personnel decisions are critical to preserving or changing the culture of a college. Any culture-enhancing strategy must consider how processes of recruitment, selection, and retention can produce the desired results. Selective recruitment of new faculty and staff can maintain cultural values or introduce different assumptions and beliefs to the institution (Van Maanen and Barley 1984) and shape the future development of the culture.

Institutional culture, particularly shared values and key events from the institutional saga, may affect the clarity and focus of search processes (Kolman et al. 1987).

Similarly, the types of students who matriculate are influenced by institutional culture. As with faculty and staff, it is important to attract students whose values, aspirations, and expectations are compatible with the values and attitudes of the institution.

7. *Institutional policies and practices are culture driven and culture bound.*

Certain themes have emerged from the historical accounts of institutional agents, usually the president, who orchestrated significant changes (e.g., taking over control of athletics in the early 1900s at Swarthmore, Wabash, and Hanover). These reports, romanticized somewhat, have similar elements; however, the meanings that they had within each institutional context were different. Thus, the transferability of policies and practices from one college to another, or from business to higher education, is problematic.

8. *Culture-driven institutional policies and practices may denigrate the integrity and worth of certain groups.*

The link between culture and performance is sometimes tenuous (Wilkins and Ouchi 1983). That is, some aspects of institutional culture (e.g., artifacts like architecture) may be irrelevant to the performance of faculty and students. Norms, language, and routine practices, however (e.g., decision making), may be debilitating for one or more groups of people (e.g., women, people of color). For example, culture may serve to perpetuate the status quo and hinder social and economic mobility (Carnoy and Levin 1985; Kempner 1988). Cultural processes in community colleges studied (Weis 1985) were racist and based on social class and reflected more of the culture of the surrounding "community of poverty" than of the institution.

Normative behavior and institutionalized practices can be demeaning to some individuals or groups. For example, under certain conditions, an appropriate metaphor for faculty behavior is cannibalism. Administrators increase resources (or salary) at the expense of other units or colleagues. During conversations with friends at other institutions, some faculty become hypercritical of colleagues in their home department. To the degree these behaviors fairly characterize faculty as individuals or groups, the metaphor of cannibal—although offensive—may accurately describe aspects of the institutional culture or sub-cultures.

To understand the influence of institutional culture on various groups, the relationships between social and political goals and cultural processes must be carefully examined. How many women and people of color are on the faculty and enrolled as students? How are women and people of color treated? To what degree are minority faculty and students integrated into the academic and social systems of the institution? These matters will become increasingly important as colleges and universities attempt to respond to societal needs by attracting and retaining more minority students and faculty.

9. *Institutional culture is difficult to modify intentionally.*

Anthropological perspectives suggest that institutional culture is immutable. Studies of efforts to change organizational culture have typically found that culture is not easily altered in intentional ways (Trice and Beyer 1984). Others (Ouchi and Wilkins 1985; Peters 1980; Sathe 1983) are more optimistic about the prospects for intentionally changing culture and believe that administrators can signal the need to modify beliefs by the questions they ask, what they attend to, and how they spend their time. Since faculty and students come to the institution from a wide variety of backgrounds and have different experiences; they bring different ideas, beliefs, and assumptions to the institution. These new ideas are based on previous cultural learning, exert a shaping influence, and also may promote changes in institutional culture to a greater degree than suggested by the anthropological perspective.

Institutional cultures have been changed or modified in seven ways: by creating new units/organizations, by changing clientele or staff significantly, by using a visionary/interpretative leadership style, by redefining strategy and mission, by reorganizing the institution, by using conflict in creative ways to identify cultural artifacts and differences between espoused and enacted values, and by using cataclysmic events and conditions to refocus institutional goals and priorities (Peterson et al. 1986). Other mechanisms or approaches may exist as well. The empirical support for these culture-changing mechanisms is based primarily on estimates of institutional climate rather than on actual changes in deeply held assumptions and values about the institution, the core of culture.

Culture represents how people have learned to cope with anxiety and the problems they face as a group (Ouchi and Wilkins 1985; Schein 1984, 1985). In this sense, altering institutional culture is tantamount to asking faculty and students to give up their social defenses. Thus, any institutional renewal effort must take culture into account because it "delimits efforts at change" (Ouchi and Wilkins 1985, p. 477). Administrators must consider the cultural risk (i.e., the degree of likely resistance) of any new policies or processes, such as sweeping changes in time-honored budgeting practices or commencement exercises. Attempts to purposefully manipulate culture point to one of the paradoxical qualities of culture: While difficult to change, culture is continually evolving because of ongoing interactions and the infusion of new people and new ideas. Thus, culture does change. Over time, however, the substantive changes in an institution's culture are not necessarily predictable or controllable.

10. *Organizational size (several hundred faculty and many thousands of students) and complexity work against the evolution of institutionally distinctive patterns of values and assumptions.*

Structural features, such as size and organizational complexity (Clark and Trow 1966), dilute the capacity of institutional culture to shape student and faculty behavior and hinder intentional modification of cultural properties at the institutional level. Efforts to understand the culture of a large university must consider the numerous faculty and student subcultures and the different meanings members of these groups have for institutional traditions and symbols as well as group-specific traditions and symbols. Although it is possible to redefine old ceremonials and create new traditions in large universities, efforts at institutional renewal in large universities are especially challenging because so many groups have their own traditions and idiosyncratic interpretations of activities and events.

Inquiry into Culture in Higher Education
The nature of culture (complex, mutually shaping, holistic, continually evolving, essentially tacit) suggests that traditional methods of social science research, grounded in logical positiv-

ism, are not capable of describing the multiple, overlapping layers of institutional culture.

The culture audit

Institutional culture can be analyzed by determining: the degree of consensus among members, the type of content of the culture, the congruence among its content elements, the strength in terms of its control over member behavior, its continuity over time, its distinctiveness (or belief that it is unique), and its clarity (Peterson et al. 1986, p. 125).

The purpose of a culture audit is to systematically identify artifacts, values, and institutionally relevant assumptions about matters, such as the nature of teaching and learning, the reward structure, students' efforts, relationships between faculty and students, and collaboration and cooperation in the academy (cf. National Association 1987). Techniques of inquiry are required that can gently probe manifestations of meaning, cognition, competence, and quality (Fetterman 1987). One such approach is the ethnographic culture audit (Fetterman 1987).

Ethnographic auditing enables an investigator to capture multiple realities, describe these different perspectives in ways that can be understood and appreciated by others, and provide insights into the cultural knowledge used by people to enact meaning and perform effectively under conditions of ambiguity (Chilcott 1987). An ethnographic approach also accommodates the mutually shaping influences of subcultures, values, rituals, and the physical environment (Fetterman 1987).

The ethnographic audit can be particularly powerful when conducted within a paradigm of appreciative inquiry. Appreciative inquiry, like naturalistic inquiry (Lincoln and Guba 1985), attempts to discover and understand the nature of life and meaning making within socially constructed organizations (Cooperrider and Srivastva 1987). Four principles of appreciative inquiry seem compatible with cultural perspectives:

1. Research into the sociology and psychology of institutional life should begin with appreciation. The inquirer must attempt to understand the dynamics internal to the institution as well as external factors and forces that influence the behavior of faculty, students, and administrators.
2. Research should be applicable to problems and concerns

that students and institutional agents believe are important. Cultural inquiries should be shared with members of the institution to help them better understand the context in which they live and work.
3. Research should be provocative. Studies of cultural meaning should generate alternative interpretations of the normative value system held by members of the institution and stimulate development of imaginative but moral purposes for the institution.
4. Research should be collaborative. Faculty, students, and administrators should be invited to participate in examining their culture for both epistemological as well as practical/ethical reasons (Cooperrider and Srivastva 1987; Lincoln and Guba 1985).

Techniques of inquiry for assessing institutional culture

Techniques used in ethnographic auditing include observation of participants, interviewing key informants, focus groups, expressive autobiographical interviews, and triangulation (Fetterman 1987). Physical traces, document analysis, archival searches, and recorded folktales may also be useful. Pencil-and-paper instruments (e.g., checklists, survey questionnaires) are sometimes employed as adjuncts to qualitative methods in assessing culture.

Culture auditors (e.g., administrators or faculty members) begin by identifying the basic assumptions held by various individuals (e.g., president, chief academic officer, faculty leaders) and groups (e.g., faculty by discipline, student subcultures) by which appropriate behavior at their institution is determined (Ouchi 1983). Are faculty encouraged and rewarded for pursuing individual interests or group interests? Are members of different groups (e.g., women, people of color) treated equitably, or are inappropriate differences in treatment tolerated? Attention should be given to those places in the institution where culture is most likely to assert or reveal itself, such as events and activities that mark the beginning and ending of the academic year and socialization processes for new faculty and students.

Six "life problems" common to any organization should be considered during a culture audit:

1. The affective orientation of the institution: To what de-

gree do people become emotionally bound with others in the work setting?

2. The orientation to causality: To what degree do people attribute responsibility for personal problems to others or to the system?
3. The orientation to hierarchy: To what degree do people acknowledge differences in position, role, power, and responsibility?
4. The orientation to change: To what degree do people willingly take risks and embark on new ventures?
5. The orientation to collaboration: To what degree do people work alone or with and through others?
6. The orientation to pluralism: To what degree do people in different interest groups relate to one another? (Bate 1984).

A worst-case scenario is a college in which faculty have:

...a low commitment to and involvement in the change process; a disowning of problems and an abdication of responsibility for the search for solutions; a lack of openness in confronting and dealing jointly with issues; avoidance of data gathering on the causes of problems; overcaution and a lack of decisiveness and creativity in problem solving; erection of barriers to change; and adopting an adversary position on all issues regardless of whether any potential measure of agreement may exist (Bate 1984, p. 63).

Contrast the foregoing with the descriptions of colleges with high faculty morale (Rice and Austin 1988): empowering leaders with an aggressively participatory individual style; willingness to share information; collaboration and focused support, not competition; and an intentionally designed flat organizational structure that minimizes hierarchical distinctions ("the teaching faculty/administration faculty, [a] 'family'...that sets the tone for the institution"—Council of Independent Colleges 1988, p. 19).

People define reality in metaphorical language and often draw inferences—consciously or unconsciously, set goals, make commitments, and execute plans based on the structure and experience provided by a metaphor (Lakoff and Johnson 1980). Incorporating metaphorical analysis as part of a culture audit (Owens and Steinhoff 1988) can be as simple as asking faculty and students to compare the operation and administration of the institution to some familiar object or activity ("to what would you compare the way decisions are made around here?"). What metaphors do faculty use to describe the institution (e.g., "family" or "factory")?

Consider the metaphorical paradigms used to understand institutional culture (Martin and Meyerson 1986). Colleges with an integrative culture attempt to reduce ambiguity by emphasizing consistency and consensus. One metaphor for an integrated college culture is the hologram or jungle clearing. In differentiated collegiate cultures, the metaphor may be islands of clarity, denoting consensus within but not between subcultures. A metaphor for an ambiguous institutional culture could be a web, characterizing a complex network of relationships that lacks clarity and focus for the institution as a whole. One interpretation of the metaphor of web is that although multiple positions may be taken on any given issue on a large university campus, these positions are relational and interconnected. Consensus, dissensus, or confusion may coexist simultaneously in different units. To be successful under such conditions, faculty and administrators must reflect a high degree of tolerance (even appreciation) for ambiguity.

Culture audits may be more revealing during stressful periods in the institution's history, as artifacts, values, and assumptions are invoked more often when faculty and students perceive a threat to "how things are done around here." Clashes between subcultures (between students and faculty groups, for example) and changes in leadership (a new president or dean) add stress to the workplace and often magnify certain aspects of the culture.

Culture audits are not foolproof, however. Audits often generate more questions than answers about core assumptions and the meaning of artifacts to different groups. Nevertheless, the information gathered through a culture audit promises richer understandings about institutional culture.

Need for additional research

As more people become familiar with the cultural perspective, informative studies of institutional culture and the role of subcultures in student learning and development may be produced. Cultural perspectives are especially well suited for case studies of exemplary colleges, such as the work of Rice and Austin (1988) on colleges with high faculty morale and Kuh and Schuh's study (in progress) of factors related to high-quality out-of-class experiences of students. Cultural perspectives would be particularly useful in examining the experiences of minority faculty and students in predominantly white institutions and university governance structures and processes. For example, how do traditions and ceremonials involve or alienate minority students and faculty? How is interaction across social, racial, and sex groups facilitated or hindered by cultural properties? To what degree do cultural properties (e.g., language) hinder women's full participation in institutional decision making?

Surprisingly little empirical research has been published that focuses on faculty and student groups using the concept of subculture, particularly from the point of view of anthropology. Much of the published research violates the definitions of subculture presented earlier (cf. Bolton and Kammeyer 1972; Van Maanen and Barley 1985). Perhaps examinations of faculty enclaves using cultural perspectives have been limited somewhat by the constraints imposed by existing definitions of subculture. And because culture helps define one's identity, some may view investigations into cultural properties as threatening. In any event, given the interest in interpreting life in colleges and universities using cultural perspectives (Tierney 1988), additional frameworks for examining the behavior of faculty and student groups are needed. This section briefly describes two frameworks, the clan and the occupational community, that have heuristic value for understanding faculty behavior.

Academic clans. A clan is a well-defined, institution-specific group that has existed for some time and employs relatively stable mechanisms of acculturation (Wilkins and Ouchi 1983). Clans are likely to form in settings that are relatively complex and high in uncertainty, conditions compatible with the description of colleges and universities as organized anarchies (Cohen and March 1974). Because few interesting or appealing alternatives to membership in a clan are available within the immediate setting, the clan has little competition from other groups for members' affections and attentions.

Affiliation with a clan tends to isolate faculty from other groups that hold competing views and encourages the development of a distinctive sense of identity. Relatively stable membership allows development of norms that suggest to newcomers how to behave. Because the clan is the primary locus of interaction for members, academic clans tend to develop idiosyncratic explanations and understandings of events and actions. Some clan members may develop chauvinistic attitudes toward other groups and discredit orientations that differ from their own (e.g., humanities versus business faculty, researchers versus faculty heavily involved in service). Such behavior perpetuates circular thinking and insulates the clan from ideas that are not part of the ideology on which the clan relies to interpret events and actions in the college (Weick 1983). "The result is that the members of the clan come to share a rather complex understanding of their environment, which is largely taken for granted and which they label with a special language" (Wilkins and Ouchi 1983, p. 469).

Occupational communities. Another framework for examining faculty behavior is the occupational community:

> ...*a group of people who consider themselves to be engaged in the same sort of work; whose identity is drawn from the work; who share with one another a set of values, norms, and perspectives that apply to but extend beyond work-related matters; and whose social relationships meld work and leisure* (Van Maanen and Barley 1984, p. 287).

Thus, the concept of occupational community emphasizes the pervasive influence of the occupational role on one's identity and social relationships (Gertzl 1961).

The identity or self-image derived from the occupational role is sharpened when members of the occupational community possess, or believe they possess, scarce, socially valued, and unique abilities. A pervasive, esoteric system of codes or language emerges, which also engenders a strong identity.

> *[The] common language, which arises from a similarity of tradition...facilitates mutual understanding...but, taken by itself, it is not sufficient to constitute a communal relationship.... It is only with the emergence of a consciousness of difference from third persons who speak a different language that the fact that two persons speak the same language and, in that respect, share a common situation, can lead them to a feeling of community* (Weber 1968, pp. 42–43).

The confluence of codes and community-specific language determines a group perspective on reality and influences how members of the community interpret what takes place in a college or university. For many faculty in research universities and prestigious liberal arts colleges, the language framework is defined externally (e.g., by subgroups within scholarly disciplines, such as "invisible colleges") (Crane 1972).

"Those who live within an occupational embrace find their work and leisure pursuits mixed in many ways and mixed so that where one ends and the other begins is a matter of some ambiguity" (Kanter, cited in Van Maanen and Barley 1984, p. 307). For many, the overlap between work and social relationships is a mild, sometimes unnoticed, intrusion. For some, such as residence hall staff who hold full-time, live-in positions and thus establish social relations mainly with fellow counselors (Barley 1983), the occupation becomes a "total work institution" (Goffman 1961). A circumscribed social network is more likely to evolve when faculty and staff live and work in close physical proximity. Of course, physical proximity is not a necessary or sufficient condition for melding social and work relationships (Schein 1985); however, proximity promotes and eases social interaction (Newcomb 1962).

Descriptions of faculty and student cultures have often reflected naive, simplistic understandings of the diversity of attitudes, values, structures, rules, and cultural artifacts (language, symbols, stories) common to various groups. The clan and occupational community frameworks reinforce the importance of discovering how faculty actually perform their jobs rather than emphasizing what others think they do or should be doing. And these frameworks suggest that the differences among faculty groups may be as interesting as the similarities. Frameworks compatible with the cultural perspective, such as academic clans and occupational communities, can guide research into the careers of faculty and administrators and offer a different perspective on the role of peer groups in colleges and universities in socializing faculty and students.

Summary

Cultural perspectives can be penetrating lenses for examining and understanding events in an institution and the behavior of faculty, students, and administrators. Goals, policies and procedures, routine practices, strategies, and leadership activities take on richer, more complex meanings when viewed as cultural phenomena. Traditional methods of social science research are not well suited for identifying properties of institutional culture. Qualitative methods, such as ethnographic culture audits grounded in the paradigm of appreciative inquiry, enable researchers to identify cultural properties and develop an appreciation of the holistic influence of the institution's culture.

More research is needed before the potential of cultural perspectives as analytical lenses can be evaluated. Frameworks compatible with cultural perspectives, such as clans and occupational communities, have potential for generating meaningful insights into college and university life.

REFERENCES

The Educational Resources Information Center (ERIC) Clearinghouse
on Higher Education abstracts and indexes the current literature on
higher education for inclusion in ERIC's data base and announcement
in ERIC's monthly bibliographic journal, *Resources in Education*
(RIE). Most of these publications are available through the ERIC
Document Reproduction Service (EDRS). For publications cited in this
bibliography that are available from EDRS, ordering number and price
are included. Readers who wish to order a publication should write to
the ERIC Document Reproduction Service, 3900 Wheeler Avenue,
Alexandria, Virginia 22304. (Phone orders with VISA or MasterCard
are taken at 800/227-ERIC or 703/823-0500.) When ordering, please
specify the document (ED) number. Documents are available as noted
in microfiche (MF) and paper copy (PC). Because prices are subject to
change, it is advisable to check the latest issue of *Resources in
Education* for current cost based on the number of pages in the
publication.

Adams, W. 1984. "Getting Real: Santa Cruz and the Crisis of Liberal
Education." *Change* 16 (4): 19–27.

Allaire, Y., and M.E. Firsirotu. 1984. "Theories of Organizational
Culture." *Organization Studies* 5: 193–226.

Allison, G.T. 1971. *Essence of Decision: Explaining the Cuban
Missile Crisis*. Boston: Little, Brown & Co.

Ansa, P. 1986. "Organizational Culture and Work Group Behavior:
An Empirical Study." *Journal of Management Studies* 23 (3):
347–62.

Argyris, C., and D.A. Schon. 1978. *Organizational Learning: A
Theory of Action Perspective*. Reading, Mass.: Addison-Wesley.

Arnold, D.R., and L.M. Capella. 1985. "Corporate Culture and the
Marketing Concept: A Diagnostic Instrument for Utilities." *Public
Utilities Fortnightly* 116 (8): 32–38.

Astin, A.W. 1985. *Achieving Educational Excellence*. San Francisco:
Jossey-Bass.

Astin, A.W., and K.C. Green. 1987. *The American Freshman:
Twenty-Year Trends*. Los Angeles: Univ. of California–Los
Angeles, Higher Education Research Institute. ED 279 279. 225 pp.
MF–1.07; PC not available EDRS.

Astin, A.W., and J.L. Holland. 1961. "The Environmental
Assessment Technique: A Way to Measure College Environments."
Journal of Educational Psychology 52: 308–16.

Austin, A.E., and Z.F. Gamson. 1983. *Academic Workplace: New
Demands, Heightened Tensions*. ASHE-ERIC Higher Education
Report No. 10. Washington, D.C.: Association for the Study of
Higher Education. ED 243 397. 131 pp. MF–$1.07; PC–$14.01.

Baird, L.L. 1987. "The College Environment Revisited: A Review of

Research and Theory." Paper read at the meeting of the Association for the Study of Higher Education, November, Baltimore, Maryland.

Baker, E.L. 1980. "Managing Organizational Culture." *McKinsey Quarterly*: 51–67.

Baker, F.S. 1978. *Glimpses of Hanover's Past*. Seymour, Ind.: Graessle-Mercer.

Baldridge, J.V., D.V. Curtis, G.P. Ecker, and G.L. Riley. 1977. "Alternative Models of Governance in Higher Education." In *Governing Academic Organizations*, edited by J. Baldridge and T. Deal. Berkeley, Cal.: McCutchan.

Barker, R.G. 1968. *Ecological Psychology: Concepts and Methods for Studying the Environment of Human Behavior*. Stanford, Cal.: Stanford Univ. Press.

Barker, R.G., and P.V. Gump, eds. 1964. *Big School, Small School*. Stanford, Cal.: Stanford Univ. Press.

Barley, S. 1983. "Semiotics and the Study of Occupational and Organizational Cultures." *Administrative Science Quarterly* 28: 393–413.

Basu, J.E. 1984. "Berkeley and Stanford: The Etiquette of Gentlemanly Competition." *Change* 16 (2): 32–37 +.

Bate, P. 1984. "The Impact of Organizational Culture on Approaches to Organizational Problem-solving." *Organization Studies* 5: 43–66.

Bates, R.J. 1981. "Management and the Culture of the School." In *Management of Resources in Schools*, edited by R. Bates. Geelong, Australia: Deakin Univ. Press.

———. 1984. "Toward a Critical Practice of Educational Administration." In *Leadership and Organizational Culture: New Perspectives on Administrative Theory and Practice*. Urbana: Univ. of Illinois Press.

———. 1987. "Corporate Culture, Schooling, and Educational Administration." *Educational Administration Quarterly* 23: 79–115.

Bay, C. 1962. "A Social Theory of Higher Education." In *The American College*, edited by N. Sanford. New York: John Wiley & Sons.

Becher, T. 1981. "Toward a Definition of Disciplinary Cultures." *Studies in Higher Education* 6: 109–22.

———. 1984. "The Cultural View." In *Perspectives in Higher Education*, edited by B. Clark. Berkeley: Univ. of California Press.

———. 1987. "The Disciplinary Shaping of the Profession." In *The Academic Profession*, edited by B. Clark. Berkeley: Univ. of California Press.

Becker, H.S., and B. Geer. 1960. "Latent Culture." *Administrative Science Quarterly* 5: 303–13.

Becker, H.S., B. Geer, and E.C. Hughes. 1968. *Making the Grade: The Academic Side of College Life*. New York: John Wiley & Sons.

Becker, H.S., B. Geer, E.C. Hughes, and A.L. Strauss. 1961. *Boys in White*. Chicago: Univ. of Chicago Press.

Benson, J.K. 1983. "Paradigm and Praxis in Organizational Analysis." *Research in Organizational Behavior* 5: 33–56.

Berelson, B., and G. Steiner. 1964. *Human Behavior: An Inventory of Findings*. New York: Harcourt, Brace & World.

Berger, P.L., and T. Luckmann. 1966. *The Social Construction of Reality: A Treatise in the Sociology of Knowledge*. Garden City, N.Y.: Anchor Books.

Bernier, N. 1987. "The Dean as Participant Observer." *Journal of Teacher Education* 38 (5): 17–22.

Bertalanffy, L., von. 1968. *General System Theory*. Rev. ed. New York: Braziller.

Bess, J.L. 1978. "Anticipatory Socialization of Graduate Students." *Research in Higher Education* 8: 289–317.

————. 1982. *University Organization: A Matrix Analysis of the Academic Professions*. New York: Human Services Press.

Beyer, J.M. 1981. "Ideologies, Values, and Decision Making in Organizations." In *Handbook of Organizational Design*, vol. 2, edited by P. Nystrom and W. Starbuck. New York: Oxford Univ. Press.

Biglan, A. 1973. "The Characteristics of Subject Matter in Different Academic Areas." *Journal of Applied Psychology* 57: 195–203.

Blau, P.M. 1973. *The Organization of Academic Work*. New York: John Wiley & Sons.

Boje, D.M., D.B. Fedor, and L.M. Rowland. 1982. "Mythmaking: A Qualitative Step in OD Interventions." *Journal of Applied Behavioral Science* 18: 17–28.

Bolton, C.D., and K.C.W. Kammeyer. 1967. *The University Student: A Study of Student Behavior and Values*. New Haven, Conn.: College and Univ. Press.

————. 1972. "Campus Cultures, Role Orientations, and Social Types." In *College and Student: Selected Readings in the Social Psychology of Higher Education*, edited by K. Feldman. New York: Pergamon Press.

Bowen, H.R. 1977. *Investment in Learning*. San Francisco: Jossey-Bass.

Bowen, H.R., and J.H. Schuster. 1986. *American Professors: A National Resource Imperiled*. New York: Oxford Univ. Press.

Bragg, A.K. 1976. *The Socialization Process in Higher Education*. AAHE-ERIC Higher Education Report No. 7. Washington, D.C.: American Association for Higher Education. ED 132 909. 54 pp. MF–$1.07; PC–$7.73.

Bredeson, P.V. 1987. "Languages of Leadership: Metaphor Making in Educational Administration." Paper read at a meeting of the

University Council for Educational Administration, October, Charlottesville, Virginia.

Broom, L., and P. Selznick. 1973. *Sociology: A Text with Adapted Readings*. New York: Harper & Row.

Brubacher, J.S., and W. Rudy. 1976. *Higher Education in Transition*. 3d ed. New York: Harper & Row.

Burns, J.M. 1978. *Leadership*. New York: Harper & Row.

Burns, T., and C.D. Laughlin. 1979. "Ritual and Social Power." In *The Spectrum of Ritual: A Biogenetic Structural Analysis*, edited by E. d'Aquili, C. Laughlin, and J. McManus. New York: Columbia Univ. Press.

Burrell, G., and G. Morgan. 1979. *Sociological Paradigms and Organizational Analysis*. London: Heineman.

Bushnell, J.H. 1962. "Student Culture at Vassar." In *The American College*, edited by N. Sanford. New York: John Wiley & Sons.

Cameron, K.S. 1984. "Organizational Adaptation and Higher Education." *Journal of Higher Education* 55: 122–44.

———. 1985a. *Cultural Congruence, Strength, and Type*. Working Paper. Ann Arbor: Univ. of Michigan. ED 259 627. 52 pp. MF–$1.07; PC–$7.73.

———. 1985b. "Managing Self-renewal." In *Leadership and Institutional Renewal*, edited by R.M. Davis. New Directions in Higher Education No. 49. San Francisco: Jossey-Bass.

Cameron, K.S., and D. Whetten. 1983. "Models of the Organizational Lifecycle: Applications to Higher Education." *Review of Higher Education* 6: 269–99.

Caplow, T., and R.J. McGee. 1958. *The Academic Marketplace*. New York: Basic Books.

———. 1968. "Publish or Perish." In *Organizational Careers: A Sourcebook for Theory*, edited by B. Glaser. Chicago: Aldine.

Capra, F. 1983. *The Turning Point: Science, Society, and the Rising Culture*. New York: Basic Books.

Carnegie Council on Policy Studies in Higher Education. 1980. *Three Thousand Futures: The Next Twenty Years for Higher Education*. San Francisco: Jossey-Bass.

Carnegie Foundation for the Advancement of Teaching. 1987. *A Classification of Institutions of Higher Education*. Rev. ed. Princeton, N.J.: Author.

Carnoy, M., and H. Levin. 1985. *Schooling and Work in the Democratic State*. Stanford, Cal.: Stanford Univ. Press.

Catlin, D., Jr. 1982. *Liberal Education at Yale*. Washington, D.C.: Univ. Press of America.

Chaffee, E.E. 1983. *Case Studies in College Strategy*. Boulder, Colo.: National Center for Higher Education Management Systems. ED 246 803. 282 pp. MF–$1.07; PC–$26.48.

————. 1984. "Successful Strategic Management in Small Private Colleges." *Journal of Higher Education* 55 (2): 212–41.

Chapple, E.D., and S.C. Coon. 1942. *Principles of Anthropology.* New York: Holt.

Chase, A. 1980. *Group Memory: A Guide to College and Student Survival in the 1980s.* Boston: Little, Brown & Co.

Chilcott, J.H. 1987. "Where Are You Coming From and Where Are You Going? The Reporting of Ethnographic Research." *American Educational Research Journal* 24 (2): 199–218.

Clark, B.R. 1960. *The Open Door College: A Case Study.* New York: McGraw-Hill.

————. 1963. "Faculty Culture." In *The Study of Campus Cultures,* edited by T. Lunsford. Boulder, Colo.: Western Interstate Commission on Higher Education.

————. 1970. *The Distinctive College: Reed, Antioch, and Swarthmore.* Chicago: Aldine.

————. 1972. "The Organizational Saga in Higher Education." *Administrative Science Quarterly* 17 (2): 178–84.

————. 1980. *Academic Culture.* Yale Higher Education Research Group/Report No. 42. New Haven, Conn.: Yale Univ., Institute for Social and Policy Studies.

————. 1984. *The Higher Education System: Academic Organization in Cross-national Perspective.* Berkeley: Univ. of California Press.

Clark, B.R., and M. Trow. 1966. "The Organizational Context." In *College Peer Groups: Problems and Prospects for Research,* edited by T.M. Newcomb and E.K. Wilson. Chicago: Aldine.

Clark, B.R., P. Heist, T.R. McConnell, M.A. Trow, and G. Yonge. 1972. *Students and Colleges: Interaction and Change.* Berkeley: Univ. of California, Center for Research and Development in Higher Education.

Clark, D.L. 1985. "Emerging Paradigms in Organizational Theory and Research." In *Organizational Theory and Inquiry: The Paradigm Revolution.* Beverly Hills, Cal.: Sage.

Clark, S.M., and M. Corcoran. 1986. "Perspectives on the Professional Socialization of Women Faculty." *Journal of Higher Education* 57: 20–43.

Clark, T.D. 1977. *Indiana University: Midwestern Pioneer.* Vol. 3, *Years of Fulfillment.* Bloomington: Indiana Univ. Press.

Coates, J. 1986. *Women, Men, and Language: A Sociolinguistic Account of Sex Differences in Language.* New York: Longman.

Cohen, A.K. 1970. "A General Theory of Subcultures." In *The Sociology of Subcultures,* edited by D. Arnold. Berkeley, Cal.: Glendessary Press.

Cohen, M.D., and J.G. March. 1974. *Leadership and Ambiguity: The American College President.* New York: McGraw-Hill.

Cohen, P.S. 1969. "Theories of Myth." *Man* 4: 337–53.

Connell, C. 1983. "Bob Jones University: Doing Battle in the Name of Religion and Freedom." *Change* 15 (4): 38–45.

Cooperrider, D.L., and S. Srivastva. 1987. "Appreciative Inquiry in Organizational Life." *Research in Organizational Change and Development* 1: 129–69.

Corbett, H.D., W.A. Firestone, and G.B. Rossman. 1987. "Resistance to Planned Change and the Sacred in School Cultures." *Educational Administration Quarterly* 23: 36–59.

Corcoran, M., and S.M. Clark. 1984. "Professional Socialization and Contemporary Career Attitudes of Three Faculty Generations." *Research in Higher Education* 20: 131–53.

Coughlin, E.K. 17 July 1985. "The 'Crits' v. The Legal Academy: Arguing a Case against the Law." *Chronicle of Higher Education*: 5–6.

Council of Independent Colleges. 1988. *Community, Commitment, and Congruence: A Different Kind of Excellence.* Washington, D.C.: Author.

Crane, D. 1972. *Diffusion of Knowledge in Scientific Communities.* Chicago: Univ. of Chicago Press.

Creswell, J.W., and J.P. Bean. 1981. "Research Output, Socialization, and the Biglan Model." *Research in Higher Education* 15: 69–91.

Cummings, K.V. 1978. "Rhode Island School of Design: The Politics of Art." *Change* 10 (6): 32–35 +.

Cunningham, D.J. 1984. "Semiotics: A New Foundation for Education?" *Contemporary Education Review* 3 (3): 411–21.

Cusick, P.A. 1987. "Introduction." *Educational Administration Quarterly* 23: 5–10.

Deal, T.E., and A.A. Kennedy. 1982. *Corporate Cultures.* Reading, Mass.: Addison-Wesley.

———. 1983. "Culture: A New Look through Old Lenses." *Journal of Applied Behavioral Science* 19: 497–505.

Deegan, W., B. Steele, and T. Thelin. 1985. *Translating Theory into Practice: Implications of Japanese Management Theory for Student Personnel Administration.* Columbus, Ohio: National Association for Student Personnel Administrators. HE 021 315. 85 pp. MF–$1.07; PC–$10.13

Dill, D.D. 1982. "The Management of Academic Culture: Notes on the Management of Meaning and Social Integration." *Higher Education* 11: 303–20.

Durkheim, E. 1933 (reprint of 1893 ed.). *The Division of Labor in Society*, translated by G. Simpson. New York: Free Press.

Ebers, M. 1985. "Understanding Organizations: The Poetic Mode." *Journal of Management* 11 (2): 51–62.

Edmond, J.B. 1978. *The Magnificent Charter: The Origin and Role of the Morrill Land-Grant Colleges and Universities*. Hicksville, N.Y.: Exposition Press.

Education Commission of the States. 1980. *Challenge: Coordination and Governance in the '80s*. Report No. 134. Denver: Author. ED 194 019. 102 pp. MF–$1.07; PC–$12.07

Elmore, R.F. 1987. "Reform and the Culture of Authority in the Schools." *Educational Administration Quarterly* 23: 60–78.

Erickson, F. 1987. "Conceptions of School Culture: An Overview." *Educational Administration Quarterly* 23: 11–24.

Etzioni, A. 1975. *A Comparative Analysis of Complex Organizations: On Power, Involvement, and Their Correlates*. Rev. ed. New York: Free Press.

Fass, P.S. 1977. *The Damned and the Beautiful: American Youth in the 1920s*. Oxford: Oxford Univ. Press.

Feldman, K.A., and T.M. Newcomb. 1969. *The Impact of College on Students*. San Francisco: Jossey-Bass.

Feldman, S. 1985. "Culture and Conformity: An Essay on Individualized Adaptation in a Centralized Bureaucracy." *Human Relations* 38 (4): 341–56.

Ferguson, M. 1980. *The Aquarian Conspiracy: Personal and Social Transformation in the 1980s*. Boston: Houghton Mifflin.

Fetterman, D. 1987. "Ethnographic Auditing: A New Approach to Evaluating Management in Higher Education." Paper read at a meeting of the American Educational Research Association, April, Washington, D.C. ED 283 839. 39 pp. MF–$1.07; PC–$5.79.

Forgas, J.P. 1985. *Language and Social Situations*. New York: Springer-Verlag.

Freedman, M.B. 1967. *The College Experience*. San Francisco: Jossey-Bass.

———. 1979. *Academic Culture and Faculty Development*. Berkeley, Cal.: Montaigne.

Frost, P., and G. Morgan. 1983. "Symbols and Sensemaking: The Realization of a Framework." In *Organizational Symbolism*, edited by L. Pondy, P. Frost, G. Morgan, and T. Dandridge. Greenwich, Conn.: JAI.

Gadamer, H. 1979. "The Problem of Historical Consciousness." In *The Interpretive Social Science*, edited by P. Rabinow and W. Sullivan. Berkeley: Univ. of California Press.

Gaff, J.G., and R.C. Wilson. 1971. "Faculty Cultures and Interdisciplinary Studies." *Journal of Higher Education* 42 (3): 186–201.

Gage, N.L. 1978. *The Scientific Basis of the Art of Teaching*. New York: Teachers College Press.

Galligani, D.J. 1984. *"Changing the Culture of the University."*

Paper presented at the annual meeting of the American Educational Research Association, New Orleans, Louisiana. ED 244 530. 70 pp. MF–$1.07; PC–$7.73.

Gamson, Z.F. 1967. "Performance and Personalism in Student-Faculty Relations." *Sociology of Education* 40: 279–301.

———. 1984. *Liberating Education*. San Francisco: Jossey-Bass.

Gard, R.E. 1970. *University-Madison-USA*. Madison: Wisconsin House Ltd.

Gardner, J.W. 1986. *The Tasks of Leadership*. Leadership Papers No. 2. Washington, D.C.: Independent Sector.

Geertz, C. 1973. *The Interpretation of Cultures*. New York: Basic Books.

Georgiou, P. 1973. "The Goal Paradigm and Notes toward a Counter Paradigm." *Administrative Science Quarterly* 18: 291–310.

Gertzl, B.G. 1961. "Determinants of Occupational Community in High-Status Occupations." *Sociological Quarterly* 2: 37–40.

Gilligan, C. 1982. *In a Different Voice: Psychological Theory and Women's Development*. Cambridge, Mass.: Harvard Univ. Press.

Gleick, J. 1987. *Chaos: Making a New Science*. New York: Viking Press.

Goffman, E. 1959. *The Presentation of Self in Everyday Life*. New York: Doubleday.

———. 1961. *Encounters*. Indianapolis: Bobbs-Merrill.

Goodlad, J.I. 1984. *A Place Called School*. New York: McGraw-Hill.

Goody, J. 1977. "Against 'Ritual': Loosely Structured Thoughts on a Loosely Defined Topic." In *Secular Ritual*, edited by S. Moore and B. Myerhoff. Netherlands: Van Gorcum.

Gordon, G.N. 1969. *The Languages of Communication*. New York: Hastings.

Gottleib, D., and B. Hodgkins. 1963. "College Student Subcultures: Their Structures and Characteristics Relative to Student Attitude Change." *School Review* 71: 266–89.

Gouldner, A.W. 1957. "Cosmopolitans and Locals." *Administrative Science Quarterly* 2: 281–306, 444–80.

Grant, G., and D. Riesman. 1978. *The Perpetual Dream: Reform and Experiment in the American College*. Chicago: Univ. of Chicago Press.

Green, E.A. 1979. *Mary Lyon and Mount Holyoke: Opening the Gates*. Hanover, N.H.: Univ. Press of New England.

Greenfield, T.B. 1973. "Organizations as Social Inventions: Rethinking Assumptions about Change." *Journal of Applied Behavioral Science* 9: 551–74.

———. 1984. "Leaders and Schools: Willfulness and Nonnatural Order in Organizations." In *Leadership and Organizational Culture: New Perspectives on Administrative Theory and Practice*, edited by T. Sergiovanni and J. Corball. Urbana: Univ. of Illinois Press.

Gregory, K. 1983. "Native-view Paradigms: Multiple Culture and Culture Conflicts in Organizations." *Administrative Science Quarterly* 28: 359–76.

Gross, T. 4 February 1978. "How to Kill a College: The Private Papers of a College Dean." *Saturday Review of Literature*: 13–21.

Gusfield, J., and D. Riesman. 1968. "Faculty Culture and Academic Careers." In *The College Student and His Culture: An Analysis*, edited by K. Yamamoto. Boston: Houghton Mifflin.

Hall, H.T. 1969. *The Hidden Dimension*. Garden City, N.Y.: Anchor Books.

———. 1976. *Beyond Culture*. Garden City, N.Y.: Anchor Books.

Handy, C. 1976. *Understanding Organizations*. London: Penguin.

Harris, M. 1968. *The Rise of Anthropological Theory*. New York: Thomas Y. Crowell.

———. 1979. *Cultural Materialism: The Struggle for a Science of Culture*. New York: Random House.

Heath, D.H. 1968. *Growing Up in College: Liberal Education and Authority.* San Francisco: Jossey-Bass.

———. 1981. "A College's Ethos: A Neglected Key to Effectiveness and Survival." *Liberal Education* 67: 89–111.

Hochbaum, J. 1968. "Structure and Process in Higher Education." *College and University* 43: 190–202.

Hoebel, E.A. 1966. *Anthropology: The Study of Man*. New York: McGraw-Hill.

Hofstede, G.L. 1981. "Culture and Organizations." *International Studies of Management and Organization* 10: 15–41.

Homans, G.C. 1950. *The Human Group*. New York: Harcourt, Brace, World.

Horowitz, H.L. 1984. *Alma Mater: Design and Experience in Ten Women's Colleges from Their Nineteenth-century Beginnings to the 1930s*. Boston: Beacon Press.

———. 1986. "The 1960s and the Transformation of Campus Cultures." *History of Education Quarterly* 26: 1–38.

———. 1987. *Campus Life: Undergraduate Cultures from the End of the 18th Century to the Present*. New York: Alfred A. Knopf.

Hossler, D. 1984. *Enrollment Management*. New York: College Board.

Howard, G.S. 1985. "Can Research in the Human Sciences Become More Relevant to Practice?" *Journal of Counseling and Development* 63: 539–44.

Hughes, E.C., H.S. Becker, and B. Geer. 1962. "Student Culture and Academic Effort." In *The American College*, edited by N. Sanford. New York: John Wiley & Sons.

Hunter, D.E., and G.D. Kuh. 1987. "The 'Write Wing': Characteristics of Prolific Contributors to the Higher Education Literature." *Journal of Higher Education* 58: 443–62.

Irwin, J. 1970. "Notes on the Present Status of the Concept of Subculture." In *The Sociology of Subculture*, edited by D. Arnold. Berkeley, Cal.: Glendessary Press.

Jacob, P.E. 1957. *Changing Values in College*. New York: Harper & Row.

Jelinek, M., L. Smircich, and P. Hirsch. 1983. "Introduction: A 'Code' of Many Colors." *Administrative Science Quarterly* 28: 331–38.

Jencks, C., and D. Riesman. 1962. "Patterns of Residential Education: A Case Study of Harvard." In *The American College*, edited by N. Sanford. New York: John Wiley & Sons.

———. 1969. *The Academic Revolution*. Garden City, N.Y.: Anchor Books.

Jensen, K. 1982. "Women's Work and Academic Culture." *Higher Education* 11: 67–83.

Kadushin, C. 1976. "Networks and Circles in the Production of Culture." *American Behavioral Scientist* 19 (6): 769–84.

Kamens, D.H.1977. "Legitimating Myths and Educational Organizations: The Relationship between Organizational Ideology and Formal Structure." *American Sociological Review* 42: 208–19.

Kanter, R.M. 1979. *Men and Women of the Corporation*. New York: Basic Books.

Katchadourian, H.A., and J. Boli. 1985. *Careerism and Intellectualism among College Students*. San Francisco: Jossey-Bass.

Katz, J., and Hartnett, R.T. 1976. *Scholars in the Making: The Development of Graduate and Professional Students*. Cambridge, Mass.: Ballinger.

Kauffman, J.F. 1980. *At the Pleasure of the Board: The Service of the College and University President*. Washington, D.C.: American Council on Education.

Keesing, R. 1974. "Theories of Culture." *Annual Review of Anthropology* 3: 73–97.

Keeton, M.T. 1971. *Models and Mavericks*. New York: McGraw-Hill.

Keeton, M., and C. Hilberry. 1969. *Struggle and Promise: A Future for Colleges*. New York: McGraw-Hill.

Keller, G. 1986. "Free at Last: Breaking the Chains That Bind Education Research." *Review of Higher Education* 10: 129–34.

Kelly, J.W. 1985. "Storytelling in High-Tech Organizations: A Medium for Sharing Culture". Paper presented at the annual meeting of the Western Speech Communication Association, February, Fresno, California. ED 254 883. 20 pp. MF–$1.07; PC–$3.85.

Kempner, K. 1988. "Faculty Culture in the Community College: Facilitating or Hindering Learning?" Paper read at a meeting of the American Educational Research Association, April 6, New Orleans, Louisiana.

Kerr, C. 1964. "The Frantic Race to Remain Contemporary." In *The Contemporary University: USA*, edited by R. Morison. Boston: Houghton Mifflin.

Kerr, C., and M.L. Gade. 1984. *The Many Lives of Academic Presidents*. Washington, D.C.: Association of Governing Boards of Universities and Colleges.

Kilmann, R.H., M. Saxton, R. Serpa, and Associates, eds. 1985. *Gaining Control of the Corporate Culture*. San Francisco: Jossey-Bass.

Kolb, D.A. 1981. "Learning Styles and Disciplinary Differences." In *The Modern American College*, edited by A. Chickering. San Francisco: Jossey-Bass.

Kolman, E., D. Hossler, M. Perko, and F. Catania. 1987. "The Influence of Institutional Culture on Presidential Selection." Paper read at a meeting of the Association for the Study of Higher Education, February, San Diego, California. ED 281 457. 15 pp. MF–$1.07; PC–$3.85.

Kramer, H.C. 1986. "Organizational Culture: Understanding Advising Systems." Paper read at a meeting of the Professional and Organizational Development Network, October 30, Somerset, Pennsylvania. ED 285 441. 17 pp. MF–$1.07; PC–$3.85.

Kroeber, A.L., and C. Kluckhohn. 1952. *Culture: A Critical Review of Concepts and Definitions*. Cambridge, Mass.: Harvard Univ. Press.

Kuh, G.D. 1977. "Admissions." In *College Student Personnel Services*, edited by W. Packwood. Springfield, Ill.: Thomas.

———. 1981. *Indices of Quality in the Undergraduate Experience*. AAHE-ERIC Higher Education Report No. 4. Washington, D.C.: American Association for Higher Education. ED 213 340. 50 pp. MF–$1.07; PC–$5.79.

Kuh, G.D., and J.H. Schuh. In progress. *A Study of Factors Related to High-Quality Out-of-class Experiences of College Students*.

Kuh, G.D., J.D. Shedd, and E.J. Whitt. 1987. "Student Affairs and Liberal Education: Unrecognized Common Law Partners." *Journal of College Student Personnel* 28: 252–60.

Kuh, G.D., E.J. Whitt, and J.D. Shedd. 1987. *Student Affairs, 2001: A Paradigmatic Odyssey*. Alexandria, Va.: American College Personnel Association.

Kuhn. T.S. 1970. *The Structure of Scientific Revolutions*. 2d ed. Chicago: Univ. of Chicago Press.

Ladd, E.C., and S.M. Lipset. 1975–76. "The Ladd-Lipset Survey." *Chronicle of Higher Education*.

Lakoff, G., and M. Johnson. 1980. *Metaphors We Live By*. Chicago: Univ. of Chicago Press.

Lane, J. 1985. "Academic Profession in Academic Organizations." *Higher Education* 14: 241–68.

Langer, S.K. 1953. *Feeling and Form*. New York: Scribner & Sons.

Langland, E., and W. Gove. 1981. *A Feminist Perspective in the Academy: The Difference It Makes*. Chicago: Univ. of Chicago Press.

Leemon, T.A. 1972. *The Rites of Passage in a Student Culture*. New York: Teachers College Press.

Levine, D.O. 1986. *The American College and the Culture of Aspiration, 1915–1940*. Ithaca, N.Y.: Cornell Univ. Press.

Levi-Strauss, C. 1973. *Anthropologie Structurale Deux*. Paris: Librairie Plon.

Lewin, K. 1936. *Principles of Topological Psychology*. New York: McGraw-Hill.

———. 1951. *Field Theory in Social Science*. New York: Harper & Row.

Light, D. 1974. "The Structure of Academic Professions." *Sociology of Education* 47: 2–28.

Lincoln, Y.S. 1986. "A Future-Oriented Comment on the State of the Profession." *Review of Higher Education* 10: 135–42.

———, ed. 1985. *Organizational Theory and Inquiry: The Paradigm Revolution*. Beverly Hills, Cal.: Sage.

Lincoln, Y.S., and E. Guba. 1985. *Naturalistic Inquiry*. Beverly Hills, Cal.: Sage.

Lodahl, J.B., and G. Gordon. 1972. "The Structure of Scientific Fields and the Functioning of University Graduate Departments." *American Sociological Review* 37: 57–72.

London, H. 1978. *The Culture of a Community College*. New York: Praeger.

Louis, M.R. 1980. "Surprise and Sense Making: What Newcomers Experience in Entering Unfamiliar Organizational Settings." *Administrative Science Quarterly* 25: 226–51.

———. 1983. "Organizations as Culture-bearing Milieux." In *Organizational Symbolism*, edited by L. Pondy, P. Frost, G. Morgan, and T. Dandridge. Greenwich, Conn.: JAI.

———. 1985. "An Investigator's Guide to Workplace Culture." In *Organizational Culture*, edited by P. Frost and Associates. Beverly Hills, Cal.: Sage.

Lunsford, T.F. 1970. "Authority and Ideology in the Administrated University." In *The State of the University: Authority and Change*, edited by C.E. Kruytbosch and S.L. Nessinger. Beverly Hills, Cal.: Sage.

MacDonald, G.B., ed. 1973. *Five Experimental Colleges*. New York: Harper & Row.

Malinowski, B. 1961. *Argonauts of the Western Pacific*. London: Oxford Univ. Press.

Manning, K. 1987. "Rituals and Meaning on a College Campus." Mimeographed. Bloomington: Indiana Univ.

March, J.G., and H. Simon. 1958. *Organizations*. New York: John Wiley & Sons.

Marshak, R.E. 1981. "Open Access, Open Admissions, Open Warfare, Part One." *Change* 13 (8): 12–19 + .

Martin, J. 1982. "Stories and Scripts in Organizational Settings." In *Cognitive Social Psychology*, edited by A. Hastorf and A. Isen. New York: Elsevier North Holland.

Martin, J., M.S. Feldman, M.J. Hatch, and S.B. Sitkin. 1983. "The Uniqueness Paradox in Organizational Stories." *Administrative Science Quarterly* 28: 438–53.

Martin, J., and D. Meyerson. 1986. "Organizational Cultures and the Denial, Channeling, and Acceptance of Ambiguity." Paper read at a meeting of the American Psychological Association, August, Washington, D.C. ED 272 804. 44 pp. MF–$1.07; PC–$5.79.

Martin, J., and M. Powers. 1983. "Truth or Corporate Propaganda: The Value of a Good War Story." In *Organizational Symbolism*, edited by L.R. Pondy, P.M. Frost, G. Morgan, and T.C. Dandridge. Greenwich, Conn.: JAI.

Martin, J., and C. Siehl. 1983. "Organizational Culture and Counterculture: An Uneasy Symbiosis." *Organizational Dynamics* 12 (2): 52–64.

Masland, A.T. 1982. "Simulators, Myth, and Ritual in Higher Education." Paper presented at the annual meeting of the Association for Institutional Research, May, Denver, Colorado. ED 220 048. 34 pp. MF–$1.07; PC–$5.79.

———. 1985. "Organizational Culture in the Study of Higher Education." *The Review of Higher Education* 8 (2): 157–68.

Mead, M. 1978. *Culture and Commitment*. Garden City, N.Y.: Anchor Books.

Meadows, P. 1967. "The Metaphors of Order: Toward a Taxonomy of Organization Theory." In *Sociological Theory: Inquiries and Paradigms*, edited by L. Gross. New York: Harper & Row.

Meister, J.S. 1982. "A Sociologist Looks at Two Schools: The Amherst and Hampshire Experiences." *Change* 14 (2): 26–34.

Merton, R.K. 1963. *Social Theory and Social Structure*. New York: Free Press.

Metzger, W.P. 1987. "The Academic Profession in the United States." In *The Academic Profession*, edited by B. Clark. Berkeley: Univ. of California Press.

Meyer, J.W. 1984. "Organizations as Ideological Systems." In *Leadership and Organizational Culture: New Perspectives on*

Administrative Theory and Practice, edited by T. Sergiovanni and J. Corbally. Urbana: Univ. of Illinois Press.

Meyer, J., and B. Rowan. 1985. "Institutionalized Organizations: Formal Structure as Myth and Ceremony." *American Journal of Sociology* 83 (2): 340–63.

Miles, M.B., and A.M. Huberman. 1984. *Qualitative Data Analysis: A Sourcebook of New Methods*. Beverly Hills, Cal.: Sage.

Millett, J.D. 1962. *The Academic Community*. New York: McGraw-Hill.

Mitchell, B.A. 1987. "Modes for Managing the Assistant Principalship: Sex Differences in Socialization, Role Orientation, and Mobility of Public Secondary School Assistant Principals." Ph.D. dissertation, Univ. of Pennsylvania.

Mitchell, D.E. 1984. "Culture and Community: The Authority of Myth and Metaphor." Paper presented at the annual meeting of the American Educational Research Association, New Orleans, Louisiana.

Mitroff, I. 1983a. "Archetypal Social Systems Analysis: On the Deeper Structure of Human Systems." *Academy of Management Review* 8: 387–97.

————. 1983b. *Stakeholders of the Organizational Mind: Toward a New View of Organizational Policy*. San Francisco: Jossey-Bass.

Mitroff, I., and R. Kilmann. 1978. *Methodological Approaches to Social Sciences*. San Francisco: Jossey-Bass.

Mitzman, B. 1979. "Reed College: The Intellectual Maverick." *Change* 11 (6): 38–43.

Moore, S., and B.G. Myerhoff. 1977. "Secular Ritual: Forms and Meanings." In *Secular Ritual*, edited by S. Moore and B. Myerhoff. Netherlands: Van Gorcum.

Morgan, G. 1980. "Paradigms, Metaphors, and Puzzle-solving in Organizational Theory." *Administrative Science Quarterly* 25 (4): 605–22.

————. 1986. *Images of Organizations*. Beverly Hills, Cal.: Sage.

Morgan, G., P. Frost, and L. Pondy. 1983. "Organizational Symbolism." In *Organizational Symbolism*, edited by L. Pondy, G. Morgan, and T. Dandridge. Greenwich, Conn.: JAI.

Morrill, P.H., and E.R. Spees. 1982. *The Academic Profession: Teaching in Higher Education*. New York: Human Sciences Press.

Morris, P. 1983. "Walk through History on Campus." *Southern Living* 18: 82–87.

Myerhoff, B. 1977. "We Don't Wrap Herring in a Printed Page: Fusion, Fictions, and Continuity in Secular Ritual." In *Secular Ritual*, edited by S. Moore and B. Myerhoff. Netherlands: Van Gorcum.

National Association of Student Personnel Administrators. 1987. *A

Perspective on Student Affairs. Iowa City: American College Testing Program.

Nelson, D.T. 1961. *Luther College: 1861–1961*. Decorah, Iowa: Luther College Press.

Newcomb, T.M. 1962. "Student Peer-group Influence." In *The American College*, edited by N. Sanford. New York: John Wiley & Sons.

Newcomb, T.M., K.E. Koenig, R. Falacks, and D.P. Warwick. 1967. *Persistence and Change: Bennington College and Its Students after 25 Years*. New York: John Wiley & Sons.

Nollen, J.S. 1953. *Grinnell College*. Iowa City: State Historical Society.

Ouchi, W.G. 1980. "Markets, Bureaucracies, and Clans." *Administrative Science Quarterly* 25: 129–41.

———. 1981. *Theory Z*. Reading, Mass.: Addison-Wesley.

———. 1983. "Theory Z: An Elaboration of Methodology and Findings." *Journal of Contemporary Business* 11: 27–41.

Ouchi, W., and A. Wilkins. 1985. "Organizational Culture." *Annual Review of Sociology* 11: 457–83.

Owens, R.G., and C.R. Steinhoff. 1988. "Toward a Theory of Organizational Culture." Paper read at a meeting of the American Educational Research Association, April 8, New Orleans, Louisiana.

Pace, C.R. 1972. *Education and Evangelism: A Profile of Protestant Colleges*. New York: McGraw-Hill.

———. 1974. *Demise of Diversity: A Comparative Profile of Eight Types of Institutions*. New York: McGraw-Hill.

Pace, C.R., and G.G. Stern. 1958. "An Approach to the Measurement of Psychological Characteristics of College Environments." *Journal of Educational Psychology* 49: 269–77.

Palmer, P.J. 1987. "Community, Conflict, and Ways of Knowing." *Change* 19 (5): 20–25.

Parlett, M.R. 1977. "The Department as a Learning Milieu." *Studies in Higher Education* 2: 173–81.

Parsons, T., and G. Platt. 1973. *The American University*. Cambridge, Mass.: Harvard Univ. Press.

Pascale, R., and A. Athos. 1981. *The Art of Japanese Management: Applications for American Executives*. New York: Warner Books.

Patton, M.Q. 1980. *Qualitative Evaluation Methods*. Beverly Hills, Cal.: Sage.

Peckham, H.H. 1967. *The Making of the University of Michigan: 1817–1967*. Ann Arbor: Univ. of Michigan Press.

Pervin, L.A. 1968. "The College as a Social System: Student Perception of Students, Faculty, and Administration." *Journal of Educational Research* 61: 281–84.

Peters, T.J. 1980. "Management Systems: The Language of the Organizational Character and Competence." *Organizational Dynamics* 9: 2–26.

Peters, T.J., and R.H. Waterman, Jr. 1982. *In Search of Excellence: Lessons from America's Best Run Companies*. New York: Harper & Row.

Peterson, M.W., K.S. Cameron, L.A. Mets, P. Jones, and D. Ettington. 1986. *The Organizational Context for Teaching and Learning: A Review of the Research Literature*. Ann Arbor, Mich.: National Center for Research to Improve Postsecondary Teaching and Learning. ED 287 437. 120 pp. MF–$1.07; PC–$12.07.

Peterson, R.E., and C. Smith. 1979. *Migration of College Students: Preliminary Analysis of Trends in College Student Migration*. Washington, D.C.: Department of Health, Education, and Welfare. ED 167 038. 14 pp. MF–$1.07; PC–$3.85.

Pettigrew, A. 1979. "On Studying Organizational Cultures." *Administrative Science Quarterly* 24: 570–81.

Philips, S.U. 1980. "Sex Differences and Language." *Annual Review of Anthropology* 9: 523–44.

Pondy, L.R. 1978. "Leadership as a Language Game." In *Leadership: Where Else Can We Go*? edited by M.W. McCall, Jr., and M.M. Lombardo. Durham, N.C.: Duke Univ. Press.

Pondy, L.R., and I.I. Mitroff. 1979. "Beyond Open System Models of Organization." In *Research in Organizational Behavior*, vol. 1, edited by B. Staw. Greenwich, Conn.: JAI.

Porto, B.L. 1984. "The Small College Experience: Not for Students Only." *Liberal Education* 70: 229–30.

Radcliffe-Brown, A. 1952. *Structure and Function in Primitive Society*. London: Oxford Univ. Press.

Redinbaugh, L.D., and D.F. Redinbaugh. 1983. "Theory Z Management at Colleges and Universities." *Educational Record* 64 (1): 26–30.

Rice, R.E., and A.E. Austin. 1988. "High Faculty Morale: What Exemplary Colleges Do Right." *Change* 20 (2): 51–58.

Riesman, D. 1981a. "The Evangelical Colleges: Untouched by the Academic Revolution." *Change* 13 (1): 13–20.

———. 1981b. *On Higher Education*. San Francisco: Jossey-Bass.

Riesman, D., and C. Jencks. 1962. "The Viability of the American College." In *The American College*, edited by N. Sanford. New York: John Wiley & Sons.

Rossi, I., and E. Higgins. 1980. "The Development of Theories of Culture." In *People in Culture*, edited by I. Rossi. New York: Praeger Press.

Ruscio, K.P. 1987. "Many Sectors, Many Professions." In *The Academic Profession*, edited by B. Clark. Berkeley: Univ. of California Press.

Salmans, S. 7 January 1983. "New Vogue: Company Culture." *New York Times.*

Sanford, R.N. 1962a. "The Developmental Status of the Freshman." In *The American College*, edited by N. Sanford. New York: John Wiley & Sons.

———. 1962b. "Higher Education as a Field of Study." In *The American College*, edited by N. Sanford. New York: John Wiley & Sons.

———. 1967. *Where Colleges Fail: A Study of the Student as a Person.* San Francisco: Jossey-Bass.

Sapienza, A.M. 1985. "Believing Is Seeing: How Culture Influences the Decisions Top Managers Make." In *Gaining Control of the Corporate Culture*, edited by R. Kilmann, M. Saxton, R. Serpa, and Associates. San Francisco: Jossey-Bass.

Sarton, M. 1961. *The Small Room.* New York: W.W. Norton.

Sathe, V. 1983. "Implications of Corporate Culture: A Manager's Guide to Action." *Organizational Dynamics* 12 (2): 5–23.

Schein, E.H. 1968. "Organizational Socialization and the Profession of Management." *Industrial Management Review* 9: 1–15.

———. 1984. "Coming to a New Awareness of Organizational Culture." *Sloan Management Review* 25 (2): 3–16.

———. 1985. *Organizational Culture and Leadership.* San Francisco: Jossey-Bass.

Schwartz, H., and S. Davis. 1981. "Matching Corporate Culture and Business Strategy." *Organizational Dynamics* 10: 30–48.

Schwartz, P., and J. Ogilvy. 1979. *The Emergent Paradigm: Changing Patterns of Thought and Belief.* Menlo Park, Cal.: SRI Analytical Report No. 7, Values and Lifestyles Program.

Scott, R.A. 1978. *Lords, Squires, and Yeomen: Collegiate Middle Managers and Their Organizations.* AAHE-ERIC Higher Education Report No. 7. Washington, D.C.: American Association for Higher Education. ED 165 641. 83 pp. MF–$1.07; PC–$10.13.

Scott, W. 1965. *Values and Organizations: A Study of Fraternities and Sororities.* Chicago: Rand McNally.

Sergiovanni, T.J. 1984. "Leadership as Cultural Expression." In *Leadership and Organizational Culture: New Perspectives on Administrative Theory and Practice*, edited by T.J. Sergiovanni and J.E. Corbally. Urbana: Univ. of Illinois Press.

Siehl, C., and J. Martin. 1982. "The Concept of Culture." Paper presented at the ICA/SCA conference on interpretive approaches to organizational community, Alta, Utah.

Smircich, L. 1983. "Concepts of Culture and Organizational Analysis." *Administrative Science Quarterly* 28: 339–58.

Snow, C.P. 1959. *The Two Cultures and the Scientific Revolution.* Cambridge: Cambridge Univ. Press.

————. 1964. *The Two Cultures: A Second Look*. Cambridge: Cambridge Univ. Press.

Snyder, B.R. 1971. *The Hidden Curriculum*. New York: Alfred A. Knopf.

Stern, G.G. 1970. *People in Context*. New York: John Wiley & Sons.

Sturner, W.F. 1972. "Environmental Code: Creating a Sense of Place on the College Campus." *Journal of Higher Education* 43: 97–103.

Tagiuri, R., and G.H. Litwin, eds. 1968. *Organizational Climate: Exploration of a Concept*. Boston: Harvard Graduate School of Business.

Taylor, F.W. 1911. *Principles of Scientific Management*. New York: Harper & Row.

Taylor, W. 1984. "Organizational Culture and Administrative Leadership in Universities." In *Leadership and Organizational Culture: New Perspectives on Administrative Theory and Practice*, edited by T. Sergiovanni and J. Corbally. Urbana: Univ. of Illinois Press.

Tewksbury, D.G. 1965. *The Founding of American Colleges and Universities before the Civil War*. New York: Anchor Books.

Thelin, J.R., and J. Yankovich. 1987. "Bricks and Mortar: Architecture and the Study of Higher Education." In *Higher Education: Handbook of Theory and Research*, vol. 3, edited by J. Smart. New York: Agathon.

Tierney, W.G. 1983. "Governance by Conversation: An Essay on the Structure, Function, and Communicative Codes of a Faculty Senate." *Human Organization* 42: 172–77.

————. 1985. "The Cultural Context of Time Management in Higher Education." Boulder, Colo.: National Center for Higher Education Management Systems. ED 270 027. 26 pp. MF–$1.07; PC–$5.79.

————. 1987. "The Semiotic Aspects of Leadership." Paper read at a meeting of the Association for the Study of Higher Education, November, Baltimore, Maryland.

————. 1988. "Organizational Culture in Higher Education: Defining the Essentials." *Journal of Higher Education* 59: 2–21.

Toennies, F. 1957. *Community and Society*, translated by P. Loomis. East Lansing: Michigan State Univ. Press.

Trice, H.M. 1984. "Rites and Ceremonials in Organizational Culture." In *Perspectives on Organizational Sociology: Theory and Research*, vol. 4, edited by S. Bacharach and S. Mitchell. Greenwich, Conn.: JAI.

Trice, H.M., J. Belasco, and J. Alutto. 1969. "The Role of Ceremonials in Organizational Behavior." *Industrial and Labor Relations Review* 23: 40–51.

Trice, H.M., and J. Beyer. 1984. "Studying Organizational Cultures through Rites and Ceremonials." *Academy of Management Review* 9: 653–69.

Trippet, B.K. 1982. *Wabash on My Mind*. Crawfordsville, Ind.: Wabash College.

Tuma, N., and A. Grimes. 1981. "A Comparison of Models of Role Orientations of Professionals in a Research-oriented University." *Administrative Science Quarterly* 26: 187–206.

Turner, V., and E. Turner. 1985. *On the Edge of the Bush: Anthropology as Experience*. Tucson: Univ. of Arizona Press.

Vaill, P.B. 1984. "The Purposing of High-Performing Systems." In *Leadership and Organizational Culture: New Perspectives on Administrative Theory and Practice*, edited by T. Sergiovanni and J. Corbally. Urbana: Univ. of Illinois Press.

Valentine, K., et al. 1985. "Understanding an Organization through Oral Traditions: No Kinks, Snakes, or Whiners Need Apply." Paper presented at the annual meeting of the Western Speech Communication Association, February, Fresno, California. ED 258 311. 37 pp. MF–$1.07; PC–$5.79.

van Gennep, A. 1960. *The Rites of Passage*. Chicago: Univ. of Chicago Press.

Van Maanen, J. 1976. "Breaking In: Socialization to Work." In *Handbook of Work, Organization, and Society*, edited by R. Dubin. Chicago: Rand McNally.

———. 1978. "People Processing: Strategies of Organizational Socialization." *Organizational Dynamics*: 19–36.

———. 1979. "The Fact of Fiction in Organizational Ethnography." *Administrative Science Quarterly* 24: 539–50.

———. 1984. "Doing Old Things in New Ways: The Chains of Socialization." In *College and University Organization: Insights from the Behavioral Sciences*, edited by J. Bess. New York: New York Univ. Press.

———. 1987. "Managing Education Better: Some Thoughts on the Management of Student Cultures in American Colleges and Universities." Paper presented at a meeting of the Association for Institutional Research, May, Kansas City, Missouri.

Van Maanen, J., and S.R. Barley. 1984. "Occupational Communities: Culture and Control in Organizations." *Research in Organizational Behavior* 6: 287–365.

———. 1985. "Cultural Organization: Fragments of a Theory." In *Organizational Culture*, edited by P.J. Frost et al. Beverly Hills, Cal.: Sage.

Van Maanen, J., and E.H. Schein. 1979. "Toward a Theory of Organizational Socialization." In *Research in Organizational Behavior*, vol. 1, edited by B.M. Staw. Greenwich, Conn.: JAI.

Veysey, L.R. 1965. *The Emergence of the American University*. Chicago: Univ. of Chicago Press.

Wallace, A.F.C. 1970. *Culture and Personality*. New York: Random House.

Wallace, W.C. 1966. *Student Culture: Social Structure and Continuity in a Liberal Arts College*. Chicago: Aldine.

Walsh, W.B. 1973. *Theories of Person-Environment Interaction: Implications for the College Student*. Iowa City: American College Testing Program.

Warren, J.R. 1968. "Student Perceptions of College Subcultures." *American Educational Research Journal* 5: 213–32.

Weber, M. 1968. *Economy and Society: An Outline of Interpretive Sociology*. New York: Bedminster.

Weick, K.E. 1976. "Educational Organizations as Loosely Coupled Systems." *Administrative Science Quarterly* 21: 1–18.

————. 1979. *The Social Psychology of Organizing*. Reading, Mass.: Addison-Wesley.

————. 1980. "Loosely Coupled Systems: Relaxed Meanings and Thick Interpretations." Ithaca, N.Y.: Cornell Univ.

————. 1983. "Contradictions in a Community of Scholars: The Cohesion-Accuracy Tradeoff." *Review of Higher Education* 20: 23–33.

————. 1985. "Sources of Order in Underorganized Systems: Themes in Recent Organizational Theory." In *Organizational Theory and Inquiry: The Paradigm Revolution*, edited by Y. Lincoln. Beverly Hills, Cal.: Sage.

Weis, L. 1985. *Between Two Worlds: Black Students in an Urban Community College*. Boston: Routlege & Kegan Paul.

Wells, H.B. 1980. *Being Lucky: Reminiscences and Reflections*. Bloomington: Indiana Univ. Press.

Wilkins, A.L. 1983. "The Culture Audit: A Tool for Understanding Organizations." *Organizational Dynamics* 12 (2): 24–38.

Wilkins, A., and W. Ouchi. 1983. "Efficient Cultures: Exploring the Relationship between Culture and Performance." *Administrative Science Quarterly* 28: 468–81.

Williams, S. 1985. "The Architecture of the Academy." *Change* 17 (2): 14–30+.

Wyer, J.C. 1982. "Theory Z—The Collegial Model Revisited: An Essay Review." *Review of Higher Education* 5: 111–17.

Yamamoto, K., ed. 1968. *The College Student and His Culture: An Analysis*. Boston: Houghton Mifflin.

Yinger, J.M. 1970. "Contraculture and Subculture." In *Sociology of Subcultures*, edited by D. Arnold. Berkeley, Cal.: Glendessary Press.

Zwerling, L.S. 1988. "The Miami-Dade Story." *Change* 20 (1): 10–23.

INDEX

ASHE-ERIC HIGHER EDUCATION REPORTS

Since 1983, the Association for the Study of Higher Education (ASHE) and the ERIC Clearinghouse on Higher Education at the George Washington University have cosponsored the ASHE-ERIC Higher Education Report series. The 1988 series is the seventeenth overall, with the American Association for Higher Education having served as cosponsor before 1983.

Each monograph is the definitive analysis of a tough higher education problem, based on thorough research of pertinent literature and institutional experiences. After topics are identified by a national survey, noted practitioners and scholars write the reports, with experts reviewing each manuscript before publication.

Eight monographs (10 monographs before 1985) in the ASHE-ERIC Higher Education Report series are published each year, available individually or by subscription. Subscription to eight issues is $60 regular; $50 for members of AERA, AAHE, and AIR; $40 for members of ASHE (add $10.00 for postage outside the United States).

Prices for single copies, including 4th class postage and handling, are $15.00 regular and $11.25 for members of AERA, AAHE, AIR, and ASHE ($10.00 regular and $7.50 for members for 1985 to 1987 reports, $7.50 regular and $6.00 for members for 1983 and 1984 reports, $6.50 regular and $5.00 for members for reports published before 1983). If faster postage is desired for U.S. and Canadian orders, add $1.00 for each publication ordered; overseas, add $5.00. For VISA and MasterCard payments, include card number, expiration date, and signature. Orders under $25 must be prepaid. Bulk discounts are available on orders of 15 or more reports (not applicable to subscriptions). Order from the Publications Department, ASHE-ERIC Higher Education Reports, The George Washington University, One Dupont Circle, Suite 630, Washington, D.C. 20036-1183, or phone us at 202/296-2597. Write for a publications list of all the Higher Education Reports available.

1988 ASHE-ERIC Higher Education Reports

1. The Invisible Tapestry: Culture in American Colleges and Universities
   George D. Kuh and Elizabeth J. Whitt

1987 ASHE-ERIC Higher Education Reports

1. Incentive Early Retirement Programs for Faculty: Innovative Responses to a Changing Environment
   Jay L. Chronister and Thomas R. Kepple, Jr.

2. Working Effectively with Trustees: Building Cooperative Campus Leadership
   Barbara E. Taylor

3. Formal Recognition of Employer-Sponsored Instruction: Conflict and Collegiality in Postsecondary Education
   Nancy S. Nash and Elizabeth M. Hawthorne

4. Learning Styles: Implications for Improving Educational Practices
   Charles S. Claxton and Patricia H. Murrell

5. Higher Education Leadership: Enhancing Skills through Professional Development Programs
   Sharon A. McDade

6. Higher Education and the Public Trust: Improving Stature in Colleges and

Universities
Richard L. Alfred and Julie Weissman

7. College Student Outcomes Assessment: A Talent Development
Perspective
Maryann Jacobi, Alexander Astin, and Frank Ayala, Jr.

8. Opportunity from Strength: Strategic Planning Clarified with Case
Examples
Robert G. Cope

1986 ASHE-ERIC Higher Education Reports

1. Post-tenure Faculty Evaluation: Threat or Opportunity?
Christine M. Licata

2. Blue Ribbon Commissions and Higher Education: Changing Academe
from the Outside
Janet R. Johnson and Lawrence R. Marcus

3. Responsive Professional Education: Balancing Outcomes and
Opportunities
Joan S. Stark, Malcolm A. Lowther, and Bonnie M.K. Hagerty

4. Increasing Students' Learning: A Faculty Guide to Reducing Stress
among Students
Neal A. Whitman, David C. Spendlove, and Claire H. Clark

5. Student Financial Aid and Women: Equity Dilemma?
Mary Moran

6. The Master's Degree: Tradition, Diversity, Innovation
Judith S. Glazer

7. The College, the Constitution, and the Consumer Student: Implications
for Policy and Practice
Robert M. Hendrickson and Annette Gibbs

8. Selecting College and University Personnel: The Quest and the Questions
Richard A. Kaplowitz

1985 ASHE-ERIC Higher Education Reports

1. Flexibility in Academic Staffing: Effective Policies and Practices
Kenneth P. Mortimer, Marque Bagshaw, and Andrew T. Masland

2. Associations in Action: The Washington, D.C., Higher Education
Community
Harland G. Bloland

3. And on the Seventh Day: Faculty Consulting and Supplemental Income
Carol M. Boyer and Darrell R. Lewis

4. Faculty Research Performance: Lessons from the Sciences and Social
Sciences
John W. Creswell

5. Academic Program Reviews: Institutional Approaches, Expectations, and
Controversies
Clifton F. Conrad and Richard F. Wilson

6. Students in Urban Settings: Achieving the Baccalaureate Degree
Richard C. Richardson, Jr., and Louis W. Bender

7. Serving More Than Students: A Critical Need for College Student Personnel Services
   Peter H. Garland

8. Faculty Participation in Decision Making: Necessity or Luxury?
   Carol E. Floyd

1984 ASHE-ERIC Higher Education Reports

1. Adult Learning: State Policies and Institutional Practices
   K. Patricia Cross and Anne-Marie McCartan

2. Student Stress: Effects and Solutions
   Neal A. Whitman, David C. Spendlove, and Claire H. Clark

3. Part-time Faculty: Higher Education at a Crossroads
   Judith M. Gappa

4. Sex Discrimination Law in Higher Education: The Lessons of the Past Decade
   J. Ralph Lindgren, Patti T. Ota, Perry A. Zirkel, and Nan Van Gieson

5. Faculty Freedoms and Institutional Accountability: Interactions and Conflicts
   Steven G. Olswang and Barbara A. Lee

6. The High-Technology Connection: Academic/Industrial Cooperation for Economic Growth
   Lynn G. Johnson

7. Employee Educational Programs: Implications for Industry and Higher Education
   Suzanne W. Morse

8. Academic Libraries: The Changing Knowledge Centers of Colleges and Universities
   Barbara B. Moran

9. Futures Research and the Strategic Planning Process: Implications for Higher Education
   James L. Morrison, William L. Renfro, and Wayne I. Boucher

10. Faculty Workload: Research, Theory, and Interpretation
    Harold E. Yuker

1983 ASHE-ERIC Higher Education Reports

1. The Path to Excellence: Quality Assurance in Higher Education
   Laurence R. Marcus, Anita O. Leone, and Edward D. Goldberg

2. Faculty Recruitment, Retention, and Fair Employment: Obligations and Opportunities
   John S. Waggaman

3. Meeting the Challenges: Developing Faculty Careers*
   Michael C.T. Brookes and Katherine L. German

4. Raising Academic Standards: A Guide to Learning Improvement
   Ruth Talbott Keimig

*Out-of-print. Available through EDRS.

*Out-of-print. Available through EDRS.

Dear Educator,

I welcome the ASHE-ERIC monograph series. The series is a service to those who need brief but dependable analyses of key issues in higher education.

(Rev.) Theodore M. Hesburgh, C.S.C.

President Emeritus, University of Notre Dame

Order Form

Quantity   Amount

_____ Please enter my subscription to the 1988 ASHE-ERIC Higher Education Reports at $60.00, 25% off the cover price.   _____

_____ Please enter my subscription to the 1989 ASHE-ERIC Higher Education Reports at $60.00.   _____

_____ Outside U.S., add $7.50 for postage per series.   _____

Individual reports are available at the following prices:

1988 and forward, $15.00 each.   1983 and 1984, $7.50 each.

1985 to 1987, $10.00 each.   1982 and back, $6.50 each.

Please send me the following reports:

_____ Report No. ____ (_____)   _____

_____ Report No. ____ (_____)   _____

_____ Report No. ____ (_____)   _____

SUBTOTAL: _____

Optional U.P.S. Shipping ($1.00 per book) _____

TOTAL AMOUNT DUE: _____

NOTE: All prices subject to change.

Name _____

Title _____

Institution _____

Address _____

_____

City _____ State _____ ZIP _____

Phone _____

Signature _____

☐ Check enclosed, payable to ASHE.   ☐ Purchase order attached.

☐ Please charge my credit card:

         ☐ VISA   ☐ MasterCard (check one)

Expiration date _____

ASHE   **ERIC**®

Send to: ASHE-ERIC Higher Education Reports
The George Washington University
One Dupont Circle, Suite 630, Dept. G4
Washington, D.C. 20036-1183